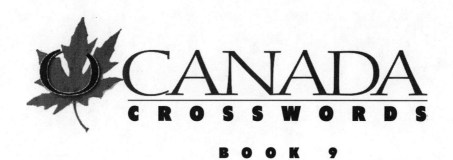

O CANADA CROSSWORDS

CROSSWORDS

BOOK 9

BOOK 9

BARBARA OLSON
DAVE MACLEOD

75 Themed Daily-Size Crosswords

NIGHTWOOD EDITIONS

Nightwood Editions
773 Cascade Crescent
Gibsons, BC
V0N 1V9
www.nightwoodeditions.com

Nightwood Editions acknowledges financial support from the Government of Canada through the Book Publishing Industry Development Program and the Canada Council for the Arts, and from the Province of British Columbia through the British Columbia Arts Council and the Book Publisher's Tax Credit.

Library and Archives Canada Cataloguing in Publication*

O Canada crosswords.

Bks. 1–7 written by Kathleen Hamilton. Bk. 8 written by Barbara Olson and Dave Macleod. Bk. 9. written by Dave Macleod and Barbara Olson.
Contents: Bk. 1. 115 great Canadian crosswords – bk. 2. 50 giant weekend-size crosswords – bk. 3. 50 more giant weekend crosswords – bk. 4. 50 incredible giant weekend crosswords – bk. 5. 50 fantastic weekend crosswords – bk. 6. 50 great weekend-size crosswords – bk. 7. 50 wonderful weekend-size crosswords – bk. 8. 75 themed daily-sized crosswords – bk. 9. 75 themed daily-sized crosswords.
ISBN-10: 1-894404-02-5 (bk. 1 : pbk.).—ISBN-10: 1-894404-04-1 (bk. 2 : pbk.).—
ISBN-10: 1-894404-20-3 (bk. 5 : pbk.).—ISBN-10: 0-88971-206-9 (bk. 6).—
ISBN-10: 0-88971-218-2 (bk. 7).—-ISBN-13: 978-0-88971-217-1 (bk. 8).—
ISBN-13: 978-0-88971-225-6 (bk. 9)

1. Crossword puzzles. 2. Canada—Miscellanea. I. Hamilton, Kathleen, 1942–
II. Olson, Barbara, 1963– III. Macleod, Dave, 1951–

GV1507.C7H35 2000   793.73'2   C 009-10576X-

Contents

1 Cool Cuisine

ACROSS

1 Part of ASA
5 ___ alai
8 Scans, as a debit card
14 Like a failed Canadian Idol, maybe
16 Nielsen of *Airplane*
17 Cool Cuisine quip, part 1
18 To a degree
19 Without a chance, in hickspeak
20 *Norma Rae* director Martin
22 "All right!"
23 They: Fr.
25 Niagara-on-the-Lake honouree
27 Cool Cuisine quip, part 2
34 Place for date squares?
35 Took another take
36 ___ *in King Arthur's Court* (1995 film)
37 Band booking
39 Twenty Questions aid
40 Gambler's state
43 Where one might get a draft
46 Cool Cuisine quip, part 3
48 Up ___ good
49 Invoice encl.
50 US pollution control grp.
53 Writer Jaffe
55 Whistler Blackcomb visitors
60 Nary a soul
62 Cool Cuisine, conclusion
64 Place to see a polar bear
65 Log-in datum
66 Made a fly fly
67 How-___ (tyro's tips)
68 Whole bunch

DOWN

1 Memo abbr.
2 Sockeye alternative
3 "___ pronounce you . . ."
4 Lucy's love
5 Like Miss America's crown
6 Response to a doctor
7 "___ one am not . . ."
8 Go like a boa
9 Lost it
10 Enabler of WWW access
11 Child's work
12 Many Newfoundlanders' motherland
13 Rummy groups
15 Do graphic art
21 Guesser's suffix
24 Doe's dear
26 Got soaked
27 Phony
28 Martini garnish
29 Edit
30 Tot's transport
31 T, for one
32 Lone Ranger's sidekick
33 Hearing aide: Abbr.
34 Water-to-wine locale
38 Rocks in rings
41 Give it one's all
42 Ticked off
44 Grinds one's teeth
45 Hide-and-seek cheater
47 Newsworld's Newman
50 Tolkien tree creatures
51 Piglet's pal
52 Peek ending
54 In ___ (stuck)
56 Fleming and McEwan
57 Series ender: Abbr.
58 Poem of Coleridge's mariner
59 Crock-Pot conconction
61 1969 Bed-In participant
63 "___ Beso" (Anka hit)

2 | *Android's Puzzle*

ACROSS

1 Canada's econ. indicator
4 Church alcove
8 Famed sci-fi author Isaac
14 Leave speechless
15 Labour heavily
16 Mt. McKinley's native name
17 Intervening stretch
19 Make a choice
20 His skeleton has gears and pulleys
22 First fratricide victim
23 London art gallery
24 Leaves in stitches?
27 Waterlogged lowland
28 ___ Aviv
31 Big name on the rails
32 The rain in Spain
35 Naïve
37 Popular see-through kids' toy of the '60s
40 Taste some
41 CSIS reps
42 Article in *Le Monde*
43 Leary's drug
44 Seek office
46 Canter or trot
48 Hockey "enforcer"
50 City turf holders
54 Cyborg from the future
58 Raspy
60 Godforsaken
61 Specialized lingos
62 "___ Tu" (1974 hit song)
63 School of the future?
64 Collection of short stories by 8-Across
65 '70s British band ___ Music
66 Publicity, slangily

DOWN

1 Powerful type of ray
2 Nerdy guy
3 Hippie's sign
4 Lead-in to boy or girl
5 Delicate ballet position
6 Like an ape
7 Opt, with "to"
8 Extra, in ads
9 Come across as
10 Old Peruvians
11 Boxing's fight of the night
12 Like Methuselah
13 Nice life
18 Don Cherry's focus: Abbr.
21 Sicilian volcano: Var.
25 Zins are dry, red ones
26 Did nothing
27 ___ *Attraction* (1987 film)
29 SASE, for one
30 Lindsay of tabloids
32 Name on a fridge
33 Attempt something
34 Play for a sap
35 Mischief maker
36 Short smoke
38 Chicane shape
39 Chain of hills
40 Warm greeting
44 The Joker portrayer Cesar
45 For him and her
47 Be like a bad headache
49 Boss, with "around"
50 Square-dance partner
51 Arcade-game maker
52 Unplugged
53 Like Zorba
55 This, in Tijuana
56 Pop quiz, for one
57 A bit too interested
58 "Bali ___"
59 1967 NHL Rookie of the Year

3 | *Not Again!*

ACROSS

1 Canada-wide: Abbr.
5 UFO shape, often
9 "This is going to be very bad!"
14 Turkish title: Var.
15 Go up: Abbr.
16 One who might want your blood
17 *Lou Grant* paper, with "The"
18 Organizing mismatched footwear?
20 Chat with the cats
22 Exposed
23 Belief
24 Echo in a tiny valley?
28 Prickly irritant
29 Egg dip, at Easter
30 MacGraw of *Love Story*
31 Dodge
35 Corps group
39 Sign on a windshield at a car lot?
43 Beginner
44 Fallback position
45 Doctor's org.
46 Unwelcome letters on a cheque
49 Hot wheels of the '50s
51 Pin for the donkey at a children's party?
55 CN stop
57 Whales no longer kept at the Vancouver Aquarium
58 You, to Yvette
59 Hasty dental procedure?
62 Sports car feature
65 ___ time (soon enough)
66 Move, in realtor-speak
67 *Coup d'*___ (glance)
68 Straw houses
69 Aches and pains, to a GP
70 Paris airport

DOWN

1 King Cole of song
2 Wheat grower's sci.
3 More in need of a quaff
4 Blue beer maker
5 Verbally trash
6 ___ water (up the creek)
7 Use elbow grease
8 Early Greek hub
9 Dreamer's sighed words
10 March start
11 King Arthur's coveted cup
12 Psych- suffix
13 Pachy- add-on
19 Bank stamp abbr.
21 Shows weakness, in a way
24 Not fitting
25 *Whoa,* ___! (2000 Juno album winner)
26 Campbell of *Scream*
27 Lambs' locales
32 Dadaist Jean
33 ___ Monte pineapples
34 She, in São Paulo
36 Enlistment officer
37 MCC x III
38 It makes your buns bigger
40 Top-notch
41 ___'acte
42 Monastery head
47 Makes sparks fly?
48 Klinger player on *M*A*S*H*
50 "Same goes for me"
51 ___ the fridge (binges)
52 Long john toppers
53 The Ruby owner on *Corner Gas*
54 Sunday song
55 Area meas.
56 Prepare to play, in a way
60 Cry on the set
61 + on a batt.
63 Vinaigrette ingredient
64 Give in excess, as alcohol

4 *Starry, Starry Night*

ACROSS

1 Believer's suffix
4 "That's ___ need!"
8 Perch and pollock
14 Stinging arachnid
16 Got through one's head
17 Focus toward
18 William Tell, for one
19 Adjusts (to)
20 Moves it
21 Narnia's Aslan
22 Native name for Mount McKinley
24 Rapper's pal
27 Less legit, as an excuse
29 Pen point
30 Surly one
31 Attention getter
33 Takes up again, in a way
35 Carrier from a well
38 Overly prim
40 Legal degs.
41 Cattle man?
42 Was winning
43 Bridge positions
48 Salt, in *une recette*
49 Steering system part
52 Bra size
53 Plant bristles
54 Unanalyzed facts
56 Pure, as wool
59 Stag party honouree
60 Skiing style
61 Plaster and paste
62 Tend to the salad again
63 Billy, the kid?
64 Saskatoon-Regina dir.

DOWN

1 "___ Be Released" (Bob Dylan)
2 Provincial word?
3 Powwow percussion
4 ... dance on the head of ___
5 Like a warm coat
6 Wrench on a bolt, sometimes
7 Mary and Joseph's destination
8 Thrash about
9 Middle of a familiar palindrome
10 Spore spots
11 Regal inits.
12 Benz ending
13 Georgia or Northumberland: Abbr.
15 Get together, as alumni
20 Canadien NHLer, informally
23 More agile
24 ___ Rabbit
25 Meadow male
26 Archaic in a dict.
28 Charlie Brown's "bummer"
30 Cuban revolutionary Guevara
32 Verbal "psst!"
33 "Sweet!" in the '90s
34 Celtic dialect
35 Has opted to
36 Communication for the deaf: Abbr.
37 Classic Cadillac
38 Ad-free TV station
39 Street of Saint-Eustache
42 Article in Abitibi
44 Calculator
45 Deli equipment
46 Teaches after school
47 Thinly scattered
49 Occurrence in 1 of 83 pregnancies
50 *ER* actress Laura
51 Russian country house
53 Currency exchange fee
55 Arouse, as an appetite
56 Dictionary abbr.
57 ___ de Montréal
58 Written school proj.
59 Vacuum accessory

5 *Ety-mology*

ACROSS

1 Neighbour of Yemen
5 Goes bad
9 ___ at 'em
14 Sitarist Shankar
15 Threat ender
16 Any Canuck, e.g.
17 Office VIP
18 Neck part
19 Aspirations
20 In a hurry
23 Zsa Zsa's sister
24 Makes up (for)
28 Moving train sound
32 Media centre?
34 Like good garden soil
35 Ho Chi Minh's capital
36 Sentry's cry
38 Gets ready for surgery
40 Pod full of cotton
41 French setting for van Gogh works
43 "He's ___ nowhere man . . ." (Beatles)
45 Tar sands product
46 %$#&*%!! (politely)
49 Where the Knesset sits
50 Firearm made in 49-Across
51 Horse's hoof sound
58 Quit, as a job
61 Time long past
62 French bread
63 Get together
64 Tush
65 ___-Ball (arcade game)
66 Lascivious deity
67 CPR experts
68 Cause of a class struggle?

DOWN

1 Pitcher Hershiser
2 Long skirt, for short
3 Opposite of sans
4 It shows a beaver on its back
5 Security guard for hire
6 Oil of ___
7 Cookbook abbrs.
8 Soak (through)
9 Cut loose
10 Where police may take their pictures
11 Any of the Dolomites
12 Born, in Baie-Comeau
13 ER honchos
21 Devil's doings
22 Install, as carpeting
25 Fictional Hudson Bay native
26 Bacterium often in the news
27 Proficiency
28 Where wine is kept
29 Gold measure
30 Polishing stuff
31 Laid-back, personality-wise
32 Abu ___ (oil emirate)
33 Husbands of countesses
37 Persistence
39 Privates, when meeting colonels
42 Helter-___
44 Likely to loaf
47 Carmaker Ransom ___ Olds
48 Most congenial
52 Burning pile
53 Haiku, for instance
54 The "E" in QED
55 Mr. Skywalker
56 Galena and cinnabar
57 Donne was one
58 Do a diner job
59 Anecdotal collection
60 "Skedaddle!"

■ DAVE MACLEOD

6 *For Crying Out Loud*

ACROSS

1 Loss of this means extinction
8 Due from, as a bill
14 Tracy/Hepburn classic (1949)
16 Rum drink with coconut
17 Court summons
18 Brand that sucks
19 Tire or tissue layer
20 Add to the discussion
22 PC panic button
23 Right at sea: Abbr.
25 Afrikaners
27 "I'm ___ here!"
30 Mantra chants
31 Rest against
35 Dog-walker's tool
38 Loop it's best to be out of
39 Hasty flight
40 Sneeze sound
42 Not 'neath
43 Attention getters
45 Enhancing undergarment
47 First man in space Gagarin
48 TSE purchase
49 "Walk ___" (Warwick hit)
50 "Take ___" (host's request)
52 Pretense
55 Concert booster
58 Rummy variety
62 Carte start
63 Arab's water-cooled pipe
65 Worshipper
67 Winged maple fruit
68 Of concern to Ahab
69 Ahab's disability
70 God of India

DOWN

1 Steamer-trunk fasteners
2 Not for minors
3 Child of the '50s
4 Dennis the Menace, for one
5 General ___ chicken (Chinese dish)
6 Bailiwick
7 Nickname for a big guy
8 Fall colours
9 One a-courting
10 "Strange Magic" band, for short
11 Your friendly crossword constructor today
12 Lyrical tributes
13 Crack investigator?
15 Chinese Cold War ideological barrier
21 Sounds of exertion
24 Copy of an orig.
26 ___ Paulo
28 Sounds of disapproval
29 Duffer's dream
32 Deck access to below
33 Cybercafe patron
34 Trillion prefix
35 Go (along)
36 Diamond Head's island
37 Harry Potter, for one
38 What every thing is
41 "Lookee here!"
44 "Mamma ___!"
46 *Nova* network in the US
48 *The Little Mermaid* villainess
51 Spook
53 "...has ___ and hungry look": *Julius Caesar*
54 One of The Donald's exes
55 Mock words of understanding
56 Haunted-house sound
57 Apple or pear
59 Mt. Rushmore's state
60 See the sights
61 Start to meter
64 ___ Kan (dog food brand)
66 Sue Grafton's ___ *for Alibi*

7 And Sometimes Y

ACROSS

1 Bridge position
5 Catch one's sweetie by surprise
15 Sign of spring
16 It's a tight squeeze
17 Common bacterium E. ___
18 Tool used on a 40-Across
19 Serengeti scavenger
21 ___ culpa
22 Musket attachment?
23 Sunday get-togethers
27 Once, once
28 Zine
30 Flaky rock
31 Sounds of surprise
33 When to show up in court
36 Les ___-Unis
40 Barbecue meat
41 Result of a punch in the mouth
43 Shire of Rocky
44 Rocky, e.g.
46 Adjective modifier: Abbr.
48 Government centre
49 Just out
50 Currier's partner in lithography
53 Guaranteed to succeed
56 Oz man's metal
57 S, N or SW
58 Gung-ho response
61 Not suitable
66 Main ingredient in Muskol
67 Damascus, e.g.
68 "The wolf ___ the door"
69 By the beach
70 The centre of Czechoslovakia?

DOWN

1 Draw on glass
2 Call for a mate
3 She'll ring you up
4 Sturdy cord
5 Radiator sound
6 Sylvester, to Tweety
7 Up until
8 "There Is Nothing Like ___" (South Pacific)
9 Thus
10 "Puppy Love" singer
11 He's a real doll
12 Not as friendly
13 Sometimes they're cracked
14 Hägar the Horrible's dog
20 All you can carry
24 Middle of Caesar's boast
25 Defeatist's words
26 Dozer name
27 Fruity-smelling compound
28 ___ Helens, WA (1980 erupter)
29 Diva's showstopper
32 Galileo was called one
34 Wanted-poster word
35 First name in mascara
37 Feelings of isolation
38 Mah-jongg piece
39 Eject, as lava
42 NHL goalie Kolzig
45 Leb. neighbour
47 They can mean "peace" or "victory"
50 "___ far, far better thing . . .": Dickens
51 LPs, slangily
52 Start of el año
54 Vega$ actor Robert
55 CBC medium
57 TV measurement
59 Cause for a handshake
60 Dog in Beetle Bailey
62 China's ___ Piao
63 A short life's story
64 Canada Post piece: Abbr.
65 Word with naked or private

■ BARBARA OLSON

 8 *Starting With the ABCs*

ACROSS

1 Sounds from a junkyard dog
5 P-T joiner
8 Villeneuve's corner
14 April honouree?
15 Red Rose product
16 Henpecks
17 Premier McGinty, for one
19 Liable to sleep in
20 Convertibles, informally
21 Place to do one's bidding?
22 Unaware, with "out"
23 Renoir's supplies
25 Day divs.
28 Summer setting in T.O.
29 Pro foe
30 Classic preppy sweater
32 Jazzy winds
34 Kids' comment
35 Stationer's supply, and what the circled answers in this puzzle have
38 "Frankly" follower
39 Ultra-proper person
40 Discount superstore
41 Main Off! ingredient
42 Bay St. trading hub
45 Pro ___ (temporarily: Lat.)
46 Calligrapher's tools
47 Electrician, often
49 WW II turning point
51 Endurance
53 Candy coats
56 "You don't stand a chance"
57 Greek letters
58 Article in *Le Devoir*
59 Prefix with -kinesis
60 Chalet, often
61 NAFTA ctry.
62 Doesn't have ___ cent

DOWN

1 Pull felt by an astronaut
2 Nancy's presidential husband
3 Still swill
4 Layered rock
5 Cotton-swab brand
6 *60 Minutes* host, once
7 Juan or José starter
8 Cold-shoulders
9 Matador's cloak
10 Like ___ on an ape
11 Mandela's ctry.
12 Large vessel
13 *Les vacances* time
18 Reel go-with
21 Canadian Prairie poet Mandel
24 Response to a rap, maybe
25 Lang. of the Torah
26 Some VCRs
27 Reggae kin
29 Pink-slip issuer
30 U-Hauls, often
31 Dundee denials
32 Joke ending?
33 Rat-___
34 So ___ (passive comment)
35 Disease carried by ticks
36 Dutch cheese town
37 "For service in English" follower
38 42-Across, e.g.
41 Susan of *L.A. Law*
42 Staler, as a saying
43 Forgetful and then some
44 Definitely not for family viewing
46 Démodé
47 Tail motion
48 "___ man with seven wives . . ."
49 Input info
50 Shot of booze
52 Mesozoic menace
53 Stop on the tracks: Abbr.
54 TV broadcast band
55 Neighbour of Fr.
56 Giant syllable

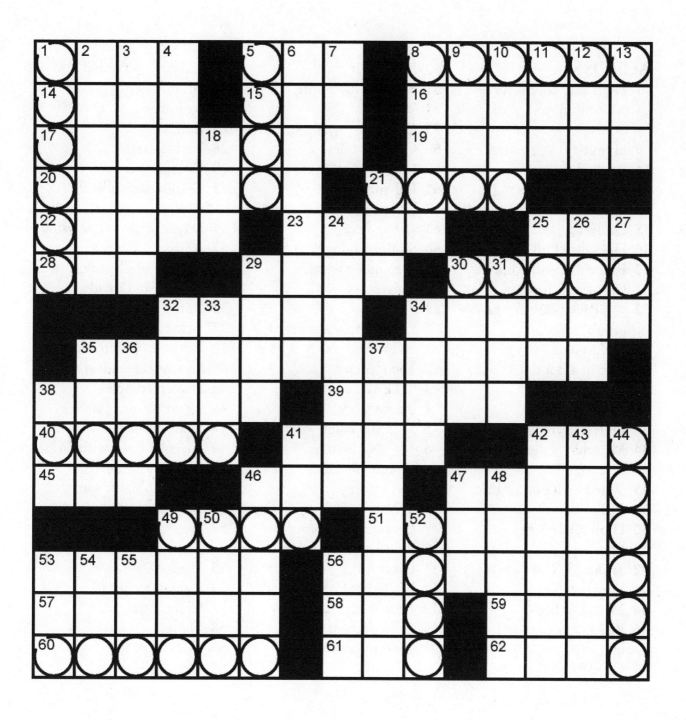

9 *Cheep Talk*

ACROSS

1 High-kite connector
4 … amount to ___ of beans
9 Hymn
14 Rocked the boat
16 Bitty bits
17 CLUCK
18 Underway
19 Hockey's Phil, familiarly
20 Farmer's field: Abbr.
21 Carpenter, for one
22 ___ Pack ('80s Liberal group)
23 QUACK
28 Part of a hot dog?
29 Startled cries
30 Cork's ctry.
31 Prefix meaning "large"
34 Miracle-___ (garden brand)
35 Word with bolt or beat
36 PEEP
40 Drains, as energy
41 Qty.
42 Strike ___ (say "cheese")
43 Film buff's stn.
44 Matter of life
45 Red hockey jersey letters in the '70s
47 GOBBLE

50 Brief "but"
53 End ___ high note
54 Whiz
55 Cut short
56 Cold outburst
59 HOOT
61 Big-time botch
62 Troubled
63 "Over here!"
64 Stopped lying?
65 Hemmer's words

DOWN

1 Colour between green and red
2 Taco topper
3 Take as one's own
4 Parrot's cry
5 Sarcastic laugh
6 "___ No Strings" (*Pinocchio* song)
7 Get smart
8 Trip-taker's drug
9 Grand instruments
10 First letter of 33-Down
11 Go from ___ B
12 A language of Thailand
13 Alta. winter setting
15 Environmental prefix
21 Kind of committee

23 "Alas, ___ Yorick!": *Hamlet*
24 Bygone days
25 Link with
26 Verbal exams
27 Colour over
28 Get louder, to Bach: Abbr.
31 Dayan with an eye patch
32 Addis ___
33 Borden's bill, slangily
34 Till key in Canada
35 Actor Johnny of *Chocolat*
37 Letter- and head- turner?
38 Paperless publication
39 Steamy, as a novel
44 Use up completely
45 Great Roman thinker
46 Eskimo shoes?
48 Goes by foot, with "it"
49 Not as well-done
50 Algonquin, for one
51 Blue Jay's coup
52 Newspaper commentary pages
55 Hockey pos.
56 Egyptian cobra
57 Certain trains
58 Owns
59 Transcript fig.
60 Mon. follower

10 Tasty Turnovers

ACROSS

1 Open up ___ of worms
5 In the future
10 Spanish parlour
14 "___ harm." (doctor's first rule)
15 *The Right Stuff* author Tom
16 Internet auctioneer
17 Peck or bushel
19 Draft-beer vessels
20 Household system of pipes
22 Zeroes in on
23 Patience-virtue link
24 ___ es Salaam
26 Marvin of Motown
27 It may come before a while
30 Beloved folk
32 Tofino tourist draw
33 It may be hidden
34 Extreme American political remedy
37 Military chaplains, informally
39 Regretful one
40 Zombie food
41 Start to dog
42 Saudi king
46 Kerouac's *Big* ___
47 "___ Mine" (Beatles)
49 Church official
50 Beating the alarm
55 ___ *and Dolls* (Brando musical)
56 It sticks up in a cave
57 Pig food
58 Kafka title, with *The*
59 At any point
60 Cross shapes
61 Penn and Lennon
62 Sunday talks: Abbr.

DOWN

1 Totalling
2 Iris covering
3 Very soon now
4 "That'll do"
5 Wage ___ of words
6 ICU site
7 Twelfth Jewish month
8 With 41-Down, feature of turnovers (and hint to the three long answers)
9 Considers
10 Highway hauler
11 Rife
12 Lingerer
13 Positive votes: Var.
18 Greek dawn goddess
21 Nag, nag, nag
25 Cape Town's ctry.
27 "___ Tu" (1974 hit song)
28 Big TV maker
29 Iliac prefix
31 Dark time for poets
32 Shout heard at birthday parties
33 End of grace
34 Playground challenge
35 It can see through any body: Abbr.
36 *Ben-*___
37 *Nova* network
38 Upscale salad item
41 See 8-Down
42 Iginla's team
43 Slot in older computers
44 "___-Skelter" (Beatles tune)
45 Things that tumble
48 Rain forest features
49 Scan for a 40-Across: Abbr.
51 Six make a fl. oz.
52 Earth as an organism
53 ___ Bator, Mongolia
54 Buddies
55 Ottawa's five percent solution: Abbr.

■ BARBARA OLSON

11 Choo Choo!

ACROSS

1 Short end of the stick
8 Healing hand, for short
11 ... ton, ta, tes, son, sa, ___
14 Weakness
15 Love letters
16 Summer hrs. in Ottawa
17 Free-fall for fun
18 Long time, informally
20 Flat sound
21 Nat'l. economic yardstick
22 Ever so dainty
23 Take ___ (get soaked)
26 King Arthur's quest
28 Rock's Bon Jovi
29 Not as ___ (rarely)
31 John of *Miracle on 34th Street*
32 CBC's ___Maria Tremonti
34 Brit's big book of words
35 Greek T
36 An X marks this spot, and it's this puzzle's theme
42 Actor Chaney, Sr. or Jr.
43 Hunky-dory
44 Whisky ___
45 Looked after
48 Corp. image-makers
50 Kiev's ctry.
51 Dude-ranch activity
53 Mirage "sightings"
55 Word origin: Abbr.
56 Latin for-instances, for short
57 Play about Capote
58 Accumulates, as laundry
60 More lewd
64 Classroom missile
65 Suffix with fruct- or sucr-
66 Writing system for the blind
67 Suffix with mock or crock
68 Mila's boy
69 Holes up at home, say

DOWN

1 Fly-catching Blue Jays: Abbr.
2 Biblical love boat?
3 Direction
4 Accomplished, once
5 Otis of elevator fame
6 Back country quads, e.g.
7 Strong soap substance
8 Walk like a wee one
9 Nutty or fruity
10 Slip a ___ (goof up)
11 St. Lawrence ___ (shipping passage)
12 Squeeze by
13 BC heritage town Fort ___
19 "The Waltz King" Johann
21 Bank offers with high credit limits
23 Slightly cracked
24 ___ fide
25 Old Roman years
26 A nephew of Scrooge
27 Transcript figs.
30 Shade for a horse
33 Record-breaking
35 Powerful puff
37 Spinster material
38 Capital on the Tiber
39 Payback promises
40 Zap
41 Sounds from a junkyard dog
45 Grassy plain
46 More affectedly cultured
47 Intercept by ambush
48 Place for a mudbath
49 Lillehammer's land
52 Minimize one's carbon footprint
54 Autobahn autos
57 Scarlett's spread
59 Kind of story or sister
60 Oil containers: Abbr.
61 In need of 8-Across, maybe
62 Jeff Lynne's band
63 Opposite of FF

■ BARBARA OLSON

12 *Crossword Construction 101*

ACROSS

1 Accessory for Frosty
6 Kid's penance, maybe
10 ___ & the Gang ('70s band)
14 Nine-___ (small golf course)
15 Orchestra's tuning instrument
16 Not, once
17 Florentine friends
18 Hot springs emanation
19 Heart charts: Abbr.
20 Crossword Construction, step #1
23 Marriage gain, for some
24 Warm over
28 Cant end?
29 Erode
30 Athlete's stats.
33 Crossword Construction, step #2
36 . . . bug in ___
38 Keats' "___ on Melancholy"
39 2% alternative, for short
40 Crossword Construction, step #3
45 Nintendo's Super ___
46 Accepted, as a challenge
47 Menu words

49 Most devious
50 Turnip's Swedish cousin
55 Crossword Construction, final step
57 Squashed ball?
60 *The King* ___
61 Actress Sagal of *8 Simple Rules*
62 TV's *Lost* island
63 Nietzsche's nada
64 Jagged-edged
65 Waist material, maybe?
66 Egg foo ___
67 Computer tower button

DOWN

1 Herring-like fishes
2 Vim rival
3 Well mate
4 Where you might find a dollop or a dash
5 Patted down a suspect
6 Roamer
7 Late news?
8 Jamaican guitarist/activist Peter
9 Rookie's mentor
10 Opposite of a bobby sock
11 Victoria's ___ Bay
12 .com alternative
13 Fleur-de-___

21 A, to Adolf
22 Prefix with physical
25 Noted US bankruptcy
26 One at ___
27 Fusses
29 City near Budapest
30 Is carried on air, as smoke
31 Conrad Black's concern, once
32 In a pout
34 Covered in dirt, in a way
35 "Till death do you part" follower
37 Singing group
41 Not ___ many words
42 A few
43 Cheque requirement
44 Work team's impediment
48 Blasting, as trumpets
50 *The Thinker* sculptor
51 Depleting, with "up"
52 They're on the road
53 "Canadian" fliers
54 Thus far
56 Prefix meaning "air" or "wind"
57 Punch-in-the-gut reaction
58 Québec's ___ d'-Or
59 Crossword solver's cry

■ DAVE MACLEOD

13 Films for the Family

ACROSS

1 Associations: Abbr.
5 Bro and sis
9 Weighed down
14 Stink to high heaven
15 Each, slangily
16 Sheeplike
17 Shout after a prank
19 Rizzo of *Midnight Cowboy*
20 Movie about Joan Crawford written by her daughter (1981)
22 Spectrum producer
23 Canada Post assignment: Abbr.
24 Variety
27 Court figure: Abbr.
28 D-H run
31 "Mayday!" signal
33 Broker's exhortation
34 Gemstone weight
36 Mindless
38 Movie musical with Fred Astaire and Leslie Caron (1955)
42 Code name
43 Teuton "thanks"
44 Lump of clay
45 ___ Na Na
48 Rapa ___ (Easter Island)

49 NHL position
52 It's sometimes furrowed
54 Hideous Tolkien beastie
56 Children's song refrain
58 Movie thriller with Mia Farrow (1968)
62 Sporty Pontiac
64 Daughter of Nicholas II
65 As ___ resort
66 Wine partner
67 "Get ___!"
68 Smacks hard
69 Study of galaxies: Abbr.
70 Bacon sizzle

DOWN

1 Pop's pop
2 Check in
3 Fishing requirement
4 Rakes off the top
5 Yegg's target
6 Popular MP3 player
7 Loud guy in the stands, often
8 Pie fight sound effects
9 Cultural identity
10 "Halt!", to a salt
11 Sack for odds and ends
12 Half of nine?
13 Conservative opening
18 Summer coolers

21 ___ Speedwagon
25 Some are groaners
26 Storm centre
29 Small salmon
30 Guy's girl
32 Most lustrous
34 DJ's assortment
35 *Dracula* director Browning
37 Birth name signifier
38 Way out
39 Tree-related
40 One of the Bobbsey twins
41 Wildebeest
42 Classic British sports car
46 Clod chopper
47 Fighting fleet
49 Brings to an end
50 Leg bones
51 The Windsors, in the news
53 Most appalling
55 ___ Major (the Great Dog constellation)
57 Building beams
59 Tipplers
60 Go off the deep end
61 River through Flanders (WW I fighting)
62 Like the Beatles, once
63 ___ *de la Cité* (Paris)

■ BARBARA OLSON

14 *Humour That's Over Your Head*

ACROSS

1 Says, in teenspeak
5 Gate fastener
10 Ultimatum ender
14 Orange flesh
15 Loud and aggressive
17 Definition of the word formed by the circled letters, part 1
19 Was no longer out
20 Canada's Harry ___ of men's fashion
21 Clue in (to)
23 Break bread
24 Stephen of *The Crying Game*
26 Leo Durocher's nickname
27 Not likely to rescue the princess
29 Saskatoon-Regina dir.
30 Prefix with dynamic
32 Like ancient inscriptions
33 Part 2 of the definition
36 Melded
39 Thicke or Eagleson
40 Temporary rage
43 Welcome gesture
45 Donovan Bailey's race
48 Springsteen's "Born in the ___"
49 Latin foot

50 Opts for
51 Gymkhana gaits
53 With no markup
54 Conclusion to the definition
58 Emergency numbers
59 Minute bit
60 Joule parts
61 Words with enter or disturb
62 ___ Penh, Cambodia

DOWN

1 Student transcript no.
2 Call at home
3 Ballot choice
4 Big spread in the city?
5 About 12 years for Fido
6 "Do I detect ___ of sarcasm?"
7 Newbie
8 Dumbo's mom, for one
9 "Yay!"
10 Terrarium residents, maybe
11 Not yet
12 Script's early heading
13 Cant finish
16 Pepper-spray targets, at times
18 2002, etched in stone

21 Snow racers
22 Canuck's sentence-enders
23 ___ Gay
25 Part of CPA: Abbr.
27 Eurasian range
28 Pirate potable
31 Some Dutch cheeses
33 French Fri.
34 Get comfortable with
35 Hush-hush
36 Loopy, in Rivière-du-Loup
37 Like many a bedroom
38 Burning on the barbecue
40 Giller Prize genre
41 Hill worker
42 Signs of withdrawal
44 Forward an email
46 Strategic move
47 Return damaged goods, say
50 Pool worker?
52 Till slot
53 Stratford, ON river
54 Fest in the West
55 "In excelsis ___"
56 Pontiac muscle car
57 Easter buy, maybe

15 O Canada

ACROSS

1 It's what's left
7 With 61-Across, what the other three theme answers represent
14 Fasten down
15 Big whoop, sarcastically
16 Like corduroy
17 They're too much
18 Tennis bad boy Nastase
19 Like a liberal arts education
20 First part of 48-Across, for short
27 Far from friendly
28 David Ogden ___ of M*A*S*H
29 "I ___ cold coming on"
32 Large in La Salle
33 It's celebrated on July 1
38 Icicle's hangout
39 "___ song of sixpence..."
40 Alex, who gives you the right answers
43 Makes steaming mad
48 Culmination of patriation in 1982
51 "It's ___ Unusual Day"
52 Canadian in 2006 Canada/US news
53 Onions' kin
57 White of the eye
59 Lawyer's request
60 Here and there
61 See 7-Across
62 Winnipeg's gold-medal speed skater Clara

DOWN

1 Add vitamins to
2 Old cry at sea
3 Shinbones
4 Cosby's "fat" guy
5 Cribbage impossibility
6 Cricket wicket
7 ___ chocolates
8 How coal is shipped
9 Fix the errata
10 Show showers
11 "___ So Fine" (Chiffons hit)
12 Bestselling number?
13 Macleod and Louisbourg, briefly
15 First-century emperor
19 Newfoundland and Labrador retriever, for two
21 Spat
22 Gen. Robert ___ of the US Civil War
23 Leslie Caron role (1958)
24 He'll save the day
25 High-tech suffix
26 Puncture sound
30 Grass skirt go-with
31 Gulf War newsman Peter
33 Dear one, in Italy
34 Cook's cooker
35 Bird beaks
36 Hindu god of fire
37 Poi base
38 List-shortening abbr.
41 Bibliographer's space-saver
42 Geisha's garb
44 Like a clock with hands
45 Round Table knight
46 French game in which kings are high
47 Goes wide of the path
49 On a scale of one ___
50 Old map abbreviation
53 Madrid Mme.
54 Feathered layer
55 One-time fill
56 Delt's neighbour
57 Sibilant silencer
58 Computer's "brain": Abbr.

16 | *Words from the Bard?*

ACROSS

1 Regard as
5 Subway meat
11 It borders It.
14 Another, in Madrid
15 Like sour grapes
16 Suffix with hero or glass
17 Narc or psych ending
18 Movie scene do-over
19 Rap's Dr. ___
20 With 37- and 55-Across, Shakespearean romantic comedy (and hint to the starred clues)
22 Humiliates
24 "You wish!"
25 Having a knack for
26 Makes aware
29 * Twister
30 Photos
31 Segment
34 Understand
35 No longer working: Abbr.
37 See 20-Across
39 Intentions
42 ___ Tin Tin
44 *Hop* ___ (Dr. Seuss)
46 Bit of gorp
47 * Courage with a swagger
50 Brought down
52 Rioted
53 The Laurentians: Abbr.
54 Tool for the can
55 See 20-Across
59 "How was ___ know?"
60 Taiwan's capital
63 Leader opposed by the Bolsheviks
64 Costello of comedy
65 Spooky TV family name
66 Between ports
67 They often get discounts: Abbr.
68 Pointed beard
69 Like healthy cheeks

DOWN

1 Apocalypse
2 Caesar's rebuke to Brutus
3 Idle of Monty Python
4 Some coffee shop orders
5 Island off Italy's boot
6 ___ spades (highest trump card, often)
7 Blotto
8 Heroine in *The Piano*
9 * Gilbert and Sullivan operetta, with "The"
10 Lettuce type
11 Worksite site for treating wounds
12 Like much junk mail
13 Handles
21 Take ___ (try some)
23 Sleep problem
25 Thoroughly enjoyed
26 EMT skill
27 180° turn, in slang
28 Beside the point
32 Amazon.com download
33 Hoodwink
36 Backless sofa
38 Hare's competitor of fable
40 West of Hollywood
41 Kind of transmission: Abbr.
43 Convention handout
45 Gridiron kick
47 Cooks from above
48 Toronto hoopster
49 * El ___ (fabled city of riches)
51 Warren Beatty/Dustin Hoffman flop (1987)
53 Muse of memory
56 Playground retort
57 Words from stubborn Scots
58 American battleship shade
61 It borders BC
62 Butter portion

■ DAVE MACLEOD

17 *What a Racket!*

ACROSS

1 It's 55-Across, like a car horn
6 Palindromic pop group
10 Pilate's "Behold!"
14 Updated, perhaps
15 Scientology's Hubbard
16 Bay of Fundy tide
17 "See? ___ you!"
18 Sometimes it's knotty
19 What winds do
20 It's 55-Across, when it's turned way up
23 After all deductions
24 Forever and a day
25 Sample, as soup
26 Comparable to a rose
28 One of Gretzky's 1,963
33 Low poker hand
36 Not care ___
38 3 on a par 5
39 Complaint about being 55-Across, perhaps
42 *The Lord of the Rings* hero
43 Down Under hoppers
44 Torso's lack
45 Get in shape
47 Short line that holds a fish hook
49 CPA's crunch them

51 French friend
52 Fairy queen of literature
55 Like an aural assault
60 *Gone With the Wind* plantation
61 Winter skating venue
62 ___-frutti
63 Somewhat
64 Ending with smack or switch
65 Miscalculated
66 "Stupid ___ stupid does"
67 Actor Bruce or Laura
68 It's 55-Across, and some call it pollution

DOWN

1 Jones, once of the Stones
2 "I'll do that"
3 Take as one's own
4 Small stream
5 Whirlpools
6 High-altitude tree
7 Wheel-shaped cheese
8 They might take years to reach maturity
9 Cause of a lack of oomph
10 Falls back
11 Common bacterium *E.* ___
12 Gator's kin

13 Gross!
21 Incursion
22 Miffed
26 ___ *Triomphe*
27 Ancient reptiles, for short
29 Coastal evergreen shrub
30 Sikorsky of aviation
31 Urban eyesore
32 Hockey's Lindsay and Green
33 Fizzling sound
34 Bubbly chocolate bar
35 Pressing need?
37 Talk, talk, talk
40 Bit of rifle ammo
41 Bill Withers hit of 1972
46 Dog-tired
48 Pay attention
50 Saw logs in the dark
52 Combining form for "mother"
53 Cádiz crafts
54 Half of a 45
55 Beliveau and Lafleur, familiarly
56 Diva's rendition
57 Charlie Brown's curse
58 ___ about (roughly)
59 Coin of the Continent
60 ___ chi ch'uan

18 *Do the Shuffle*

ACROSS

1 Early times?: Abbr.
4 Quitter's words
11 Apt. rental info
14 She "dances on the sand" in a Duran Duran song
15 Reason to take five
16 China's Chou En-___
17 Lion statues, e.g.?
19 Night school subj.
20 Blasé response
21 Hound sound
22 Evil chuckle
23 Welsh form of John
24 Forbidden fruit?
27 Q-U link
28 It's a blast
29 Put on eBay again
30 Take a ___ (try)
33 Campground shelters
34 Drama series set in a rainy playground?
36 "*Zut* ___!"
38 "So what if it's gone"
39 Noted sheep seeker
41 La-la lead-in
42 43-Down's grp., once
45 Wagers made in church?
48 Midnight Madness, e.g.
49 Barcelona bears
50 Compassionate letters
51 How *boeuf* may be served
52 Receiving the CPP
53 Bugle call signalling the end of KP duty?
56 Florida footballer, for short
57 She coined the term "domestic diva"
58 Fish tale
59 Round geom. solid
60 À la mode, literally
61 Dusk, to Donne

DOWN

1 Robin Hood, e.g.
2 Sounds of Boots
3 In order for (something to occur)
4 "___ not mistaken"
5 What Harper did before becoming prime minister
6 André's ands
7 Have a chair by, as a table
8 Hockey's Larionov and Ulanov
9 Set one's sights on
10 Maiden name preceder
11 Running, as colours
12 Most impetuous
13 Feature of French plurals
18 Name on some Canadian tabloids
22 Eruptive Mount St. ___
24 It used to be enough
25 When *The National* airs on CBC
26 Odd obsession
28 Hemingway setting
30 Rips to bits
31 Go from ___ B
32 Letter-shaped keyhole
34 Second to none
35 Romances
36 Sucks up
37 Bungle big time
40 Monty ___
42 Sweet-talk
43 Former quarterback Doug
44 Take away from
46 "___ This Mess"
47 Razzle-dazzle
48 Dine in the evening
51 Done to ___
53 Start of 28-Across
54 Beginning of time?
55 The Coneheads' show, for short

■ DAVE MACLEOD

19 *Things in Common*

ACROSS

1 Bounce off the walls
5 Woven hair
10 Tabula ___ (clean slate)
14 Lecturer's platform
15 Last movement of a sonata
16 And others: Abbr.
17 Toronto gridder
18 Computer commerce
19 Audition tape
20 Actress Tilly from Texada Island, BC
21 Leeway
23 What the goat gets
26 The March King
27 They're looking for something
29 50 Cent, e.g.
31 Fanfares
32 Hôtel manager
34 Like some martinis
35 Go fishing for eels
37 Mom-and-pop org.
40 One of an inquisitive four?
41 Sales pitch
43 A Hummer has a big one
46 Clothing styles
48 Common font
49 Psalms, for the most part
50 Result of contagious laughter, perhaps
55 Was ahead
57 Anderson of sitcoms
58 "Whole ___ Love" (Led Zeppelin)
59 Start to care?
60 A ___ apple
61 Joined, as a discussion
62 The 3 Rs: Abbr.
63 Anna May of *Shanghai Express*
64 Make happy
65 Variety

DOWN

1 Cheese town of the Netherlands
2 Stuffed animal of the '80s
3 With 37-Down, jumbled and confused
4 ___ *blanco* (polar bear)
5 Labatt, for one
6 Boeuf ___ (French roast)
7 Stifle, vis-à-vis itself: Abbr.
8 Beatnik's "Gotcha!"
9 Barbie or Ken, e.g.
10 Tea brand made "only in Canada"
11 Dined at the diner
12 Indian restaurant appetizer
13 Roberto, one-time star of the Blue Jays
22 Steam-brewed coffee
24 Wanted-poster letters
25 Base eatery
27 Kind of transmission: Abbr.
28 Smug smile
29 Unbending
30 PEI time
33 CSIS guy
36 Starter start
37 See 3-Down
38 Got nervous
39 Waxman and Purdy
40 Putting on, as a play
42 Wrestler's goal
43 Judge's reporting ban
44 Melodic composition
45 Register at the door
47 *The Fifth* ___ (CBC exposé)
51 Choice word
52 Babe in the stable
53 Kett of old comics
54 On the double, in the OR
56 Vegas cubes
59 Bumped into

20 *Water, Water, Everywhere*

ACROSS

1 "Do ___ say!"
4 Brief but
9 They're part of the process
14 Can.-US timber treaty
15 Torino toodle-oos
16 Red Square occupant
17 Haughty manner
19 Père's frère
20 Rideau Hall resident before Michaëlle
21 Post-WW II British prime minister
22 Rendezvous
23 Jackie Chan film of 1998
25 Suffix with Sudan or Japan
26 Waxman and Purdy
29 Letter letters: Abbr.
30 Where one might get a slap on the back
31 KIA model
33 It follows gab or slug
34 Plays boisterously
36 French-Canadian state?
38 Kings and queens but not jacks
39 Was into
40 Dove's cry
41 Bus rider's listings: Abbr.
42 Apt. rental info
45 Keep back, as information
48 Highlands hillside
49 Skylit chamber
50 Tubular food
54 Laughing
55 Fly-tier's supply
56 Just miss
57 Casual Friday wear
58 Not very bright
59 "…like ___ a hole in the head"
60 In your dreams
61 Kind of Cone or Cat

DOWN

1 "Aint That ___" (Cheap Trick)
2 Arrives on base, in a way
3 "Amen!"
4 Tooth trouble
5 BC CFLer
6 Small mountain lake
7 McKenzie Brothers epithet
8 Verb ending?
9 They're no workaholics
10 October's placement
11 Includes an RSVP card
12 Rubberneckers' draws
13 Regard with scorn
18 "___ me" (blackjack player's call)
21 Battery's partner
24 Noisy hubbub
26 Grocer on *The Simpsons*
27 First-class flyer's perk
28 Group of bass
31 Al-Anon recruit
32 Your, of yore
33 Apparently under a spell
34 Clothing industry, informally
35 Yonge and Bloor: Abbr.
36 King who conquered Wales
37 College fee
40 Skydived
42 Keeps under one's wing
43 Cape Breton singing family
44 Prefix meaning "earthquake"
46 Depend (on)
47 Helped do the dishes
48 "Let It Roll" rockers
51 "That ___ excuse"
52 Former PEI premier Joe
53 Words of woe
55 Health Canada's US equivalent

21 | *Over the Top*

ACROSS

1 Hurt severely
5 Old-time oath
9 Difficult ones are tight
14 Ticklish Muppet
15 Dracula portrayer Lugosi
16 "I ___ Symphony" (Supremes)
17 A closing word from Mork
18 With 62-Across, exaggerates
20 Marcel of the LA Kings
22 ___'acte (intermission)
23 Madam of 36-Across
24 Cry made with a flourish
26 Makes up (for)
28 Fine, informally
31 He played Zhivago
34 Old science magazine
35 Crop up
36 He raised Cain
40 Light gas?
41 With 4-Down and 27-Down, exaggerate
42 Guiding genius
43 Prefix meaning "within"
44 Ain't the way it should be?
45 Drooling dog of comics
46 Puts into words
48 Chin indentation
49 Get set to bite
52 Ending for refer or defer
54 *Wok With* ___ (TV chef's show)
55 CFL Hall-of-Famer Jackson
58 "Ain't That ___" (Fats Domino)
62 See 18-Across
65 Hip bones
66 Comic DeGeneres
67 Volcano near Italy's toe
68 Prevaricates
69 How grade schoolers are often grouped
70 Army eatery
71 Queue or cue, perhaps

DOWN

1 Heal
2 Jai ___
3 ___ *Angel* (1933 Mae West comedy)
4 See 41-Across
5 Subsided, as the tide
6 Type of toothpaste
7 Lotion ingredient
8 Daybreak
9 What Mickey has that Mikey doesn't?
10 Little bit of the Laurentians
11 Like some granola
12 Treasure cache
13 Sometimes they're cracked
19 Be rude toward, in a way
21 Dissenting vote
25 Equally uncommon
27 See 41-Across
28 Super-duper
29 Sign of things to come
30 Macramé unit
32 Banff visitor, often
33 In ___ (sort of)
35 Hobbyist
37 Surfer's sobriquet
38 "You wish!"
39 Bump into
47 Symbol of power
48 IV units
49 Laid-back, personality-wise
50 Before the deadline
51 ___ Gay (1945 atom bomb dropper)
53 Grannies
56 Type of cell in the news
57 Locale
59 Others, to Ovid
60 Personal appearance
61 Smooth, as a process
63 Cribbage marker
64 Switch positions

22 | *It's Music to My Ears*

ACROSS

1 Hart Trophy winner: Abbr.
4 Remain patient
10 "Get ___" (comment to a layabout)
14 Flat's lack
15 Like a loudmouth, later
16 In's influence
17 Rock band's "hot" guitar?
19 Open, as a zipper
20 Threw with effort
21 Bit of fluff
23 Frequently, to Frost
24 Part of a snobbish drummer's equipment?
29 Graceful paddler
30 State of Des Moines
31 Start to fix?
34 Brightly coloured songbird
38 Puppy owner's choice
40 Demonstrates a piano to potential buyers?
43 Ark unit
44 All told
45 Spr. setting
46 Bay St. hirees
48 Sha ___
50 Percussion instrument at a lavish party?
55 Laudatory work
56 Like some straits
57 Canadian bar
60 ___ suit (baggy '40s attire)
62 Places on a fiddle for fiddle sticks?
66 Séparatiste rally words
67 Made equal
68 Verse opener?
69 Normandy invasion site
70 Take dancing this time, say
71 Quart divs.

DOWN

1 "Monster ___"
2 Marlon's *Godfather* role
3 Canada's group of ten: Abbr.
4 Every other hurricane
5 Charged item
6 It's picked up in a bar
7 Bristol baby buggies
8 Part of CAA: Abbr.
9 Touchy (but not feely)
10 Kwik-E-Mart owner
11 Coveted Canadian statuette
12 You might meet them at a school reunion
13 Obliterates, with out
18 "I'm game!"
22 UK record label
25 Missing KP duty, maybe
26 Foot bones
27 Strike caller
28 ___ fide
31 Very softly, in music
32 Gave a tongue-lashing to
33 Extract from olives or canola
35 It touches four Great Lakes: Abbr.
36 Sierra ___, Africa
37 Founded: Abbr.
39 French direction
41 Landlocked Asian sea
42 ___ victory (made gains)
47 Lay the groundwork?
49 "When I was ___ I served . . . (*HMS Pinafore*)
50 Jackasses
51 US Food Guide word
52 Treasure follower?
53 Cut down
54 Advantage
58 Flat rate?
59 Suffix with psych- or neur-
61 Classical grp. in Ontario
63 ___ Act (Canada's Constituton of 1867)
64 Receiving the CPP
65 Suffix with fluor-

23 *Porcine Parade*

ACROSS

1 ___ double-take
4 Bad-cheque writer
9 Biblical poem
14 Hypocritical
16 Where llamas roam
17 One charged with tending to 23-, 34-, 46- and 54-Across?
18 Acknowledge tacitly
19 Photo finish
20 Commotions
22 Seed coat
23 Speculative purchase
28 Argos' gains, briefly
29 Looks with anger
30 After all deductions
31 Ending for hippo- or aero-
32 Aussie buddies
34 John Candy flick (1995)
38 Trojan War epic
39 Something under the pillow
40 *Mal de* ___ (seasickness)
41 "That ___!" (exasperated shout)
43 "___-La-La" (1974 Al Green hit)
46 Source of funding for politicians' pet projects
49 Hwy. sign at a summit
50 "Thy word is ___ unto my feet . . ." (Psalm 119)
51 More than day-old, probably
52 Little green man
54 Slangy nirvana
58 Army doc
59 Consecrating, in a way
60 Simple kind of question
61 Prominent
62 Mediocre grade

DOWN

1 Consternation
2 Progressive direction
3 The way things stand
4 Baby bouncer
5 First person in Berlin
6 Place for shigh scers?
7 Act human
8 Neckwear for SpongeBob SquarePants
9 Bamboo-eating "bear"
10 Pry
11 Builds up
12 Grassy expanse
13 Winter hrs. in Jasper
15 Like Vancouver's airport: Abbr.
21 Carry-___ (small pieces of luggage)
23 Trudge
24 "___ Said" (Neil Diamond hit)
25 Bigger
26 Newly sharpened
27 *The X-Files* extras
29 June partier
31 High-tech identifier
32 Damon or Dillon
33 "___ *du lieber!*"
34 1963 role for Liz
35 They're preceded by sirens
36 Carrot on a snowman, perhaps
37 Seethe
38 Mischief maker
41 Beaver's structure
42 Anne of Green Gables, for example
43 From the Ukraine, e.g.
44 Curtis of cosmetics
45 Get even for
47 Fashionable Calvin
48 Baccarat player's declaration
49 French-Canadian state?
51 Email command
52 *Little Women* woman
53 Golf pro Trevino
55 Lover of Lennon
56 Came down with
57 Hasten

24 | *The Whole Shootin' Match*

ACROSS

1 Get louder, in music: Abbr.
5 Holey cheese
10 Producers of goods: Abbr.
14 ___-skiing (fly-in adventure sport)
15 Land of the ancient Greeks
16 This and that
17 "I'll just be ___"
18 Smugly self-righteous
20 '70s Tupperware® slogan
22 John of England
23 Evening in Paris
24 CFL coups
25 "Hometown Proud" supermarkets
29 Diddly
33 Up the creek
36 Forage storage site
37 Store a side of beef
41 "___ you one!"
42 Places for laces
43 Fri. follower, for some
45 Salt shake
46 British novelist Barbara ___
49 Liberal-minded guy
52 Kindergarten quintet
54 Epitome of fun
60 Loss of white-collar workers
61 Half of a '70s self-help book title
62 Mortgager's security
63 One at ___
64 Peter, Paul or Mary
65 "Land of Living Skies" prov.
66 Prepare salad lettuce
67 Bitty bug

DOWN

1 Skier's retreat
2 Flipped over
3 Makes House bound?
4 Michael Moore documentary
5 Men at Work, for one
6 Pound sound
7 "Are you ___ out?"
8 Is allied (with)
9 Final word
10 Night sky events
11 Polar mass
12 Frees (of)
13 High-protein beans
19 One-time PEI premier Joe
21 How the confident do crosswords
26 Air traveller's destination
27 Like Santa's suit, presumably
28 Go over the limit, in a way
30 Cleo portrayer
31 Québecker's key
32 Old TV knob
33 Poolside potable
34 *Man ___ Mancha*
35 Very, in Versailles
37 Title of 22-Across
38 Ode opener
39 Have in hand
40 Hawke of *Dead Poets Society*
44 ___ *de tout* (It's nothing")
46 "Show me first your penny" speaker
47 Chinese-American cellist
48 What the first words of 20-, 37- and 54-Across are part of
50 ___ the hills
51 ___ *of 60*
53 Just getting by, with "out"
54 Oil qtys.
55 Diva's delivery
56 Bob and Charlotte
57 Destination of 46-Down
58 Play charades
59 Linear, as opposed to planar, briefly

■ BARBARA OLSON

25 | *Happy Endings*

ACROSS

1 Copps of the Commons, once
7 Have ___ in the matter
11 US toll hwy.
14 Election lure
15 Double-checked
17 Sevilla's country
18 "It's all over for me"
19 Kitchen Catcher pitcher
21 Roll-call call
22 Simile connector
23 "Phooey!"
25 East, in Germany
26 Film buff's channel
28 Be a fussbudget
32 Sharp, in geometry
34 Pure as the driven snow
35 Montréal comedy fest
38 Prove successful
39 Beetle Bailey's boss
40 Bowler's target
42 These, to Thérèse
43 Boundary: Abbr.
46 "It's ___-win situation"
47 Carry a balance
49 Apple or pear, to a botanist
50 Narnia confection
56 Walk tall?
57 Stretching muscle
58 "Put your money away"
59 Stampeder's rival
60 Strong soap
61 Rock blasters
62 Mick and the boys, with "The"

DOWN

1 Prefix meaning "chest"
2 Reviews, with "over"
3 Hardest level
4 Caesar's *veni*
5 Moon goddess
6 ___ all-time high
7 Mideast statesmen: Var.
8 Pago Pago native
9 Ex-NHLer Deadmarsh
10 Safecracker, slangily
11 Lunch bag sandwich fare
12 Emulates Nostradamus
13 Flop or plop opener
16 Fa-la link
20 Ipso ___
24 Just make (out)
26 Get smart, in a way
27 Grand ___ (Muslim leader)
29 "See if ___" ("It won't bug me")
30 Godfather's goons, e.g.
31 Messenger on the Hill
32 *Dilbert* co-worker
33 Verbal hesitations
35 With stylish pizazz
36 Detach, as railroad cars
37 Spiked the punch
38 Appt. keeper?
41 "It ain't gonna happen!"
43 Gets ready to Google, say
44 "Honey, ___" (Shania Twain)
45 Montréal subways
48 Makes less dull
49 Left-winger, slangily
51 Sch. hand-in, maybe
52 Actress Sedgwick
53 Gossiper's couple
54 *Etre* verb form, with "*vous*"
55 For fear that
56 Up to, quickly

26 *21st-Century Santa*

ACROSS

1 Old adders
6 Elevator button
10 Amer. military fliers
14 Kudrow of *Friends*, and others
15 "... ___ saw Elba"
16 Pkg. amount
17 Drink to leave for the 21st-century Santa
19 Modern energy source
20 "Peekaboo!" follower
21 Pick up, in a way
23 What a carpenter might drive
25 Long tales
28 Accessory for the 21st-century Santa
31 Esposito from Sault Ste. Marie
33 Pet peeve?
34 Brit's grandma
35 Changes a title
39 Snake alternatives, in a game
41 Type
42 Singer on a 2007 Canadian postage stamp
44 Sunrise direction, in Mexico
45 Wrapping used by the 21st-century Santa
50 Divided Asian land
51 Richard of *Stir Crazy*
52 Granby greeting
54 Like Family Channel movies
59 Peter Benchley page-turner
61 21st-century Santa's workshop helper
63 Baby's boo-boo
64 Word with song or dive
65 Set of values
66 Kind of apt.
67 Montgomery's Shirley
68 Auditioners' goals

DOWN

1 "___ want for Christmas ..."
2 Book jacket blurbs
3 "___ forgive those ..."
4 Joe joint
5 Mom's answer, with "Because"
6 Overmodest
7 "... ___ quit!" (ultimatum words)
8 "What have we here?" preceder
9 "Just Do It" brand
10 Open on Christmas Day
11 Scrooge's flaw
12 Wheat bristle
13 Petal pushers?
18 Second sound
22 Equally blue
24 Subordinate Claus?
26 Not together
27 Pick up, in a way
28 Success-versus-failure phrase
29 Prov. riding rep.
30 Black or Red
31 Poke with a pin
32 ___ "In your dreams!"
36 Taj ___
37 High school timetable abbr.
38 Get out of Dodge
40 BSc. or MBA
43 Second largest cont.
46 Gift for little Alice, perhaps?
47 Power of old films
48 *Orca* in 59-Across, e.g.
49 More pretentiously cultured
53 Bear in the night sky
55 Prefix meaning "outer"
56 *James and the Giant Peach* writer Roald
57 ___-dieu (prayer bench)
58 Oshawa auto output
59 Patient one, Biblically
60 Responses to a letdown
62 Secret rival

■ DAVE MACLEOD

27 *Airborne*

ACROSS

1 Niger neighbour
5 Condense
11 Tell (on)
14 Top notch
15 *Jeopardy* categories
16 Yuck!
17 Mystical poem
18 Some poles
19 Sis' sib
20 Toy-plane airscrew
22 Keaton's *Clean and ___* (1988)
24 Sense
25 Sifter
26 Forever (in poesy)
29 Eye related
31 Fittingly
32 Fern seed
33 Mire
36 Belief suffix
37 Use the other four theme answers and . . .
39 Big Web presence: Abbr.
40 Common title start
41 Some Arab leaders
42 Mr. Ferrari
43 Loretta Young role (1936)
45 One behind the other
47 Goes by

49 Dispatch
50 ___ Allan Poe
51 Toy-plane material
56 Note between fa and la
57 Cry in the outfield
59 Church recess
60 Play about Capote
61 In blackjack, it's a natural
62 Clinton alma mater
63 Dir. from Fredericton to Moncton
64 Over there
65 Reno machine

DOWN

1 Nitpick
2 Their finest, to Churchill
3 Part of A.D.
4 Cook like Colonel Sanders
5 British post-war Prime Minister
6 Waggish
7 Web page
8 What it is when the fat lady sings
9 Grand Canyon feature
10 Staff symbol
11 Toy-plane powerplant
12 Be of one mind

13 Androcles' concern
21 Dark time for poets
23 ___ *pro nobis*
25 Travel the Web
26 Redact
27 Keister
28 Toy-plane cement, maybe
29 It may be comic or grand
30 Sounds like a pigeon
32 Flay
34 Seep
35 Grab, with "onto"
37 Foolhardiness
38 Pop singer Tori
42 Lengthwise
44 Botanist Gray
45 Tricky problem
46 What makes men mean?
47 Italian, Spanish or French plague
48 Dress up
49 Pizza portion
51 Former West German capital
52 The slightest bit
53 October gem
54 Norse capital
55 Bug-spray ingredient
58 Graphic lead-in

28 *Last Gasp*

ACROSS

1 Plant bristles
5 Skin bristles
10 Bear leavings
14 Active sort
15 Pandora's release
16 Bread spread
17 Perfectly
18 Short time
20 With 53-Across, it's like 36-Across
22 Caspian, for one
23 Friend of Tarzan
24 Dawn goddess
25 Hallowe'en option
27 Baby's wrap
29 Unruly crowd
32 Gaelic
33 Colleague of Kent and Lane
34 Restrained
36 Wrapping up
41 Pipe cleaner
42 Bony prefix
43 Teeming, with "with"
46 Wine meas.
47 ___ *Weapon* (Gibson film)
48 Limber
50 ___ *favor*
51 Mineral suffix
52 Roadside stop
53 See 20-Across
58 Daytime fare
60 Gush
62 Perry Mason's creator Gardner
63 Chew scenery
64 ___ en scène (stage setting)
65 Doe, but not John
66 Lunkheads
67 Lip

DOWN

1 Summer hrs. in Halifax
2 Winter cords
3 Turkey is part of it
4 Madrid Mlle.
5 More established, in a way
6 *Dynasty* co-star Linda
7 Triangle sound
8 Scads
9 Husky rival
10 Part of USSR
11 Last pitcher, hopefully
12 Trojan War warrior
13 As yet
19 Erode, with "at"
21 Roast at summer camp
23 Sick as ___
26 Put through the paces again
28 Tube-nosed seabird
29 *Psycho* setting
30 It smells in the US
31 Post ante action, usually
34 Realm of CEOs
35 Smithies
37 Arrest
38 Abyssinia now
39 Felix Unger's obsession
40 Big name in pineapples
43 Brought up
44 Pay no heed
45 Last scene
47 Botches, with "up"
49 Prefix meaning "home"
50 Home, sometimes
54 Newspaper page, for short
55 Verne's captain
56 Trim, as hair
57 Doctrines
59 Each
61 Jazz guitarist Montgomery

29 Phone-y Excuses

ACROSS

1 "___ too!" (retort to a skeptic)
5 "Don't take ___ hard"
9 Sergeant played by Steve Martin
14 Voodoo charm
15 Breakfast spot
16 Actors Richard and Barbara
17 Director Egoyan
18 Cheque record
19 Forbidding words?
20 Cellphone excuse for ending a call, #1
23 Abu Dhabi native
24 Early 16th-century year
25 Excuse #2
30 ___-relief
32 Home loan: Abbr.
33 Do a footman's job
34 The devil's work
36 TA's milieu
38 Islamic sect
39 Spruce up the salad
42 First-rate
45 Frequent joiners, in Jonquière?
46 Excuse #3
49 "Hang it!"
50 River of Flanders
51 Excuse #4
57 Section of trees
58 D-grade
59 Fairy
60 It's beloved in Québec
61 Suffix with flex
62 Garage shopper, likely
63 Twist in a knot
64 "___ sow, so shall..."
65 "Smooth Operator" singer

DOWN

1 Amaar's title on *Little Mosque on the Prairie*
2 Chanel competitor
3 "This is ___ for Superman!"
4 Polite refusal
5 Like some potatoes or pudding
6 Carry-alls
7 Like a griper's grapes?
8 "I'm good with that"
9 Hospital buzzer site
10 Admires and then some
11 Jay seen at night
12 Don't just think
13 East in Essen
21 Barbershop request
22 Actress Lupino and others
25 "___ girl or...?"
26 Stick-on
27 Awed one
28 Dark time in Drummondville
29 Pilot predictions: Abbr.
30 When repeated, a vitamin B deficiency
31 Opposite of "sans"
35 Resident of Huron College's city
37 "Jiminy Cricket!"
40 German pastry
41 Got rid of the plug?
43 Defiant denial
44 Tied up
47 Sir Thomas More's novel about a perfect world
48 Blows one's stack
51 Put ___ writing
52 Toddler's call
53 Pocket watch chains
54 "___ Yellow Ribbon..."
55 Left one's mark?
56 "Since" in a New Year's song
57 Droop

30 Culture Club

ACROSS

1 Actress Falco of *The Sopranos*
5 With 68-Across, what each of 38-Across, 14- and 30-Down represents
12 Upscale salad herb
15 Microsoft encyclopedia
16 Like the Mackenzie, as Canadian rivers go
17 Kid with a new home
18 Tijuana ta ta
19 Walk like a peacock
21 Mountain road section
22 Light gas
23 Fold, spindle or mutilate
24 Zadora of *Hairspray*
26 Arlo, to Woody
27 Flower part
29 Crowning points
33 Folk singer Baez
35 Luau chow
37 Kipling mongoose Rikki-tikki-___
38 American flag, familiarly
42 Sets (on)
43 Chinese "way"
44 Potter's need
45 Lightly scolded
47 Never, in dialect
49 Second sight, briefly
52 CFL official
54 Don's "Coach's Corner" co-host
55 ___-Seltzer
56 Start of the MGM motto
59 Tex-Mex topping
61 Dweller on the Bering Sea
62 Model plane, e.g.
64 Michelins and Pirellis
66 Exonerated
67 Displaying cold symptoms
68 See 5-Across
69 ___ *Kleine Nachtmusik*

DOWN

1 Incite
2 Cost of union membership
3 They, in Marseilles
4 Really bothers
5 Have on
6 Become, finally
7 Nova ___
8 Something to draw from
9 Art Deco artist
10 Numbered rds.
11 Words from stubborn Scots
12 Eagleson and Thicke
13 Calgary Stampede, for one
14 British flag, familiarly
20 Magician's stage exits
23 ___ Work ('80s band)
25 When Romeo and Juliet have their balcony scene
27 N'est-ce ___?
28 Tex-Mex band ___ Lobos
30 Canadian flag, familiarly
31 Night before
32 Family girl, for short
34 Boitano rival
36 "The program's starting"
38 Jet-set jet, once
39 "___ the season . . ."
40 A Bobbsey twin
41 Noisy quarrel
46 Yearning
48 Raspy
50 *Hamlet* prop
51 Cline of country and pop
53 Diamond side
55 "Get ___!"
56 Circle segments
57 Move, in real estate lingo
58 Blueprint item
60 Di was one
61 Score after deuce, often
63 China's Chou En-___
65 Singer DiFranco

31 | *Any Body Here?*

ACROSS

1 Frat party attire, maybe
5 Some temple leaders
11 Game show hosts, briefly
14 Legendary lawman Wyatt
15 Slap the cuffs on
16 Organizers for the Vancouver Winter Games: Abbr.
17 Part of a flight
18 Top dog at work
20 Stand against a wall
22 Web page "pop-ups," e.g.
23 Not as likely to pop up
24 *Hud* Oscar winner Patricia
26 Pal of Pooh
27 Some sell bazookas
32 Neighbour of Homer
33 Dagger of yore
34 Divvy, as pizza
36 Piece of plywood
38 Fertility-lab stock
39 Cookout site
43 Some fundraisers
46 Gander, so to speak
47 Heading from Ottawa to NYC
50 New York City Prohibition-era gangster
52 Mess, with "with"
54 Moved on ice
55 "Are not!" comeback
56 Hip-hop
59 Belief of one billion
62 Reluctance to make a bold decision
65 Hatcher of *Lois and Clark*
66 Wide partner
67 Winter weasel
68 Withers on the vine
69 Serpent's warning
70 Clerk, at times
71 He's a goofball

DOWN

1 Dick Tracy's Trueheart
2 Dangerous thing to lie under
3 They're little, and they're from Mars
4 Legendary orchardist Johnny
5 "Go team!"
6 Side squared, for squares
7 Small nail
8 Hospital count
9 "Sort of" suffix
10 Gathers for later
11 Millionth of a metre
12 Stick together
13 Added points
19 Thumbs-down
21 Pet rocks, e.g.
25 Albertville article
26 "Look ___ ye leap"
27 Cleopatra's undoing
28 Genetic material
29 Side by side
30 9 ___ (cat food brand)
31 Modern alternative to Hallmark
35 Study of lifelines
37 Fraser Canyon town
40 "So long!"
41 Charged atom
42 Gave the thumbs-up
44 Maiden name preceder
45 Family girl
47 Walking sticks
48 Identical to
49 Logs, as data
51 ___ Baba
53 Came down with
56 Yukon's only law enforcers: Abbr.
57 Et ___ (and others)
58 Goes for the gold
60 Pretentious
61 Sushi bar soup
63 Make tempura
64 Up to now

32 *After U*

ACROSS

1 Dinner companion, say
5 Antioxidant used in butter: Abbr.
8 Cyndi Lauper hit
14 Expressions of disgust
15 "Merry" mois
16 King classic
17 Truck timber to a sawmill
19 Outcome
20 Camera type, briefly
21 "Nevertheless . . ."
23 Work without ___
24 Divorced parents' option
26 Fatigued action doll?
29 1998 animated bug film
30 "Got two fives for ___?"
31 Square one
33 3-Down preceder
36 Sudden deterioration
40 US toll hwy.
41 In the cooler
42 Spanish appy
43 Done to ___
44 Kind of tie or earring
46 Tailor's material buy
51 Condo or apartment
52 Carpet fibres
53 Some second degs.
56 Sigher's sensation
58 Not a turtle or crew, shirt-wise
60 Croquet player's need
61 Peachy
62 Potent prefix
63 "Dogs must be on ___"
64 CFL penalty units
65 Prez's right-hand man

DOWN

1 Dopey comments
2 "I've Got ___ in Kalamazoo"
3 Fifth day of the wk.
4 Night school subj.
5 Unlikely Genie winner
6 Actress Uta
7 Quaint denial
8 Habitual borrower
9 Hebridean "have"
10 Artificial substitute
11 He played Nick on *The Beachcombers*
12 Well-lit?
13 Tom with the Heartbreakers
18 Muhammad's 1978 ring rival
22 Severely criticize
24 "Insensitive" singer Arden
25 Store, as luggage
26 UN export and import treaty
27 Suck ___ (quit whining)
28 *The* ___ (Steve Martin/ Bernadette Peters film)
31 Sorrows
32 And so on, for short
33 Stuffed food
34 Hockey legend who always wore a black turtleneck, for short
35 Big man on campus
37 ___-Mart (place for quik pix)
38 Twenty percent
39 Suffix with neur-
43 Hun head
44 Spooky sounds
45 Lean to one side, as a ship
46 Myanmar's other name
47 7'1" NBA hoopster
48 City in northern France
49 Cornered
50 Word with "shed" or "shot"
53 Selfish refrain?
54 What cover-up covers up, maybe
55 Jennifer Jones, for one
57 Double-wide letters
59 Fallback mo.

33 Civics Class

ACROSS

1 Griffin of game shows
5 Sleep like ___
10 "Phooey!"
14 Et ___ (and others)
15 *I Pagliacci* clown
16 Olympic sword
17 One of Hamlet's options
18 Was obligated
19 Word with print or point
20 With 51-Across, the centre of Ottawa deliberations
23 Keats, to Shelley
26 "There ___ be a law!"
27 Piano trio
28 Concise concession
30 Government head
33 Company logos and such: Abbr.
34 Brando's film debut, with *The*
35 Steely Dan album (1977)
38 They're facing 30-Across during Question Period
45 Get by
46 Ran on and on
47 Spiritual music
50 In a sec
51 See 20-Across
54 Just for the heck ___
55 Late-blooming flower
56 Shania Twain or Karen Carpenter
60 Indian garment
61 Haggard of country
62 Execute perfectly, in slang
63 Bimonthly util. bill
64 Rings out
65 Hightailed it

DOWN

1 Wrestler's surface
2 "Eldorado" rockers
3 Adam's donation
4 Trouble spot of the '60s
5 Lack of belief
6 Tugs, e.g.
7 B ___ (not colour, as film)
8 ___-Honey (candy bar)
9 Calls over the back fence
10 Asylum seeker
11 Simian
12 Basic belief
13 ___ ghost (is afraid)
21 Hearty's partner
22 Give the boot to
23 Date with a doc
24 Word form for "skin"
25 Keats, for one
28 Bumbling
29 Flooring for a flat
31 Scamps
32 Bonnie of blues
36 Singer/piano man Billy
37 Artist Warhol
39 Liver-related
40 Gen ___ (one born in the early '60s)
41 It has a wick
42 Orbs
43 The earth's core, mostly
44 Kilt patterns
47 Silly person
48 Abattoir waste
49 Cathedral topper
50 What the nose knows
52 Understanding words
53 Razor name
57 Baby's seat
58 Deuce, in tennis
59 Like Methuselah

34 *What's Your Point?*

ACROSS
1 Funny noises?
6 ___ for a raise
11 Forensic drama on CBS
14 Take on, as a trait
15 When lunch break ends, for many
16 Nail-biting periods, briefly
17 French composer Erik
18 Janitor's sweeper
20 35-Down, for example
21 ___ Minor
22 "Xanadu" band, for short
23 Kindergarten art figure
25 Syllables said while covering one's ears
28 "Fingers crossed!"
29 Canadian TV awards
30 Cal. spans
31 At no time, poetically
34 Largish ensemble
35 Scoring triples
38 First name in Cuban politics
41 "¿*Cómo* ___ *usted*?"
42 Season when DST starts
45 Tried to lose?
47 ___ *Room* (preschooler's TV show, once)
50 House of hide
51 Parry Sound's hockey legend
53 Dashboard meas.
54 Dachshund draggers
56 Conclusion's beginning
57 Acrobat's security
59 Man of fable
61 Business bldg.
62 Red-nosed one
63 Khomeini was one
64 Word to the wise guy
65 Put ___ pasture
66 Pitching Hall of Famer Ryan

DOWN
1 Is ailing from
2 Plug-in connector
3 Major Houlihan's handle
4 Each
5 Salmon slabs
6 ___ New Guinea
7 One-eighty on the road
8 Turn's partner
9 Medical checkup instruction
10 Kan.'s neighbour
11 Radiator additive
12 Precinct rat
13 End of sex?
19 Finds in a museum
23 Reserved
24 Place to *faire du ski*
26 Way to run
27 Halifax hrs.
29 Sandpaper surface
32 *Nous sommes, vous* ___ , *ils sont*
33 CPR stations?
35 911 words, maybe
36 Out of the wind
37 Dr. Atkins no-no
38 Love handles, in reality
39 Say again
40 Cook onion rings
42 Husband- or wife-related
43 Public image
44 Eco-friendly letters
46 "Bye for now"
48 Acquire
49 "You're a lifesaver!"
51 Port west of Paris
52 Bone: Prefix
55 "Sometimes you feel like ___"
57 K-12 inst.
58 Roy Thompson Hall grp.
60 Word that can follow the start of 18-, 23-, 35-, 51- and 57-Across

■ DAVE MACLEOD

35 Behind Bars

ACROSS

1 '60s conflict, for short
4 Moved stealthily
9 COs on ships
14 H-shaped Greek letter
15 Nouveau ___
16 Belted constellation
17 With 41- and 65-Across, Sam Cooke hit (1960)
19 Medicinal leguminous plant
20 Cream and The Supremes
21 Like some crosswords
23 Elvis Presley hit song and movie (1957)
26 Air conditioner meas.
28 Good name for a lawyer?
29 Box-office buy: Abbr.
30 Like some exams
32 Freon or neon
34 Teen occupation
39 Taboos
41 See 17-Across
43 Taking out the garbage, e.g.
44 Pottery glaze
46 Lee who directed *Hulk*
48 English horn's cousin
49 Baby grizzly
51 Response from a doofus
53 Comics punch line?
54 Vernon Dalhart hit (1924), and what the other theme answers are each an example of
60 Produce feedback
61 Indian melodies
64 Trojan War epic
65 See 17-Across
68 "___ outta here!"
69 Share fifty-fifty
70 Modern denial (with !)
71 Sedate
72 Red as ___
73 Welcome to the villain

DOWN

1 Little amphibian
2 Valid conclusion?
3 Subject of busts
4 Mid-life event
5 ___ Tin Tin
6 Lines from the heart: Abbr.
7 You can take it on a trip
8 "At ease!" opposite
9 Skin-deep
10 Toward the back
11 It's spotted on a ranch
12 Gin go-with
13 Small bite
18 Campground initials
22 Edmonton footballers, briefly
24 Chowderhead
25 Cops, slangily
26 Mother Hubbard's lack
27 1982 film set in cyberspace
31 Herbert of Pink Panther films
33 Rock's ___ Na Na
35 However, informally
36 Sleds without runners
37 Buck back?
38 Snorkeller's haunt
40 Supported a motion
42 You hope they'll meet
45 Moon goddess
47 He's gloomy
50 "You ___!" ("Sure!")
52 Big wasp
54 Stuffed shirts
55 Get a new tenant
56 "___ boy or girl?"
57 Copycat's comment
58 Kind of centre
59 Chronic critic
62 Years abroad
63 Pepper and Preston: Abbr.
66 Molson product
67 ___ been had!

■ BARBARA OLSON

36 *I Dream of Genie*

ACROSS
1 "Gotcha!"
4 "___ Easy" (1977 Ronstadt hit)
9 Bronze winner's place
14 Sales agent, for short
15 Moved stealthily
16 "Great White North" epithet
17 Dance with a cane
18 Genie-winning director of 55-Across
20 Comics light bulb
22 More merry
23 Comedian Thomas or Foley
24 Fife companion
26 March march occasion
28 Fiona portrayer in 55-Across
30 Memo headers: Abbr.
31 Kept under one's hat
32 Group led by the host of CBC's *Vinyl Tap*
33 Tropical souvenir
36 Sun. follower
37 Super's charge: Abbr.
40 Grateful reply, in Granby
42 House of blocks
44 He won a Genie for Best Actor in 55-Across

47 Has the final word
49 Drawn out
50 French 101 verb
51 Dickens' ___ Heep (*David Copperfield*)
53 "And ___ bed"
55 Film based on Alice Munro's "The Bear Came Over the Mountain"
58 GM employee's grp.
59 Cowboy film
60 Didn't miss ___
61 ___ *vous plaît*
62 A Corleone son
63 Dos' mates
64 Golf pro Ernie

DOWN
1 Start to choke?
2 Assault à la Zinedine Zidane
3 Please or amuse
4 Suffix with phon- or phonet-
5 Heartbreaking
6 Six-winged angel
7 Certain fixers?
8 Luck ___ Irish
9 Brief but
10 Suppresses
11 Sleeps in, say

12 Actor who wore an S on his chest
13 Laundromat slot machine
19 Magic word
21 Not fer
25 Bugs to no end
27 Doing community service, say
28 Verbal dig
29 "___ Canadian!" (Molson slogan)
34 Intense zeal
35 CFB boss
37 Where one might get the draft?
38 What a bow ties, maybe
39 Daycare attendee
40 Ambled (along)
41 Neither here nor there
43 Sales slip figs.
44 Whirl about
45 Female bird with a flashy mate
46 Like a wailing cat
47 "___ Love" (The Honeydrippers)
48 Using one's arms
52 ___ to Avonlea
54 Symbols of wisdom
56 Big do
57 Freedoms' go-with: Abbr.

76

37 'Tis the Season

ACROSS

1 Very tiptops
7 How the excited go
10 *Pequod* captain
14 51 after, timewise
15 Foes of the Jays
16 Pt. of DOS
17 Gill of former CBC daytime show
18 Can't be separated from
20 BUY EVERYONE'S DRINKS
22 Perrier, to Pierre
23 System startup?
24 Byron wrote one to Napoleon
25 Busy
29 Latin lover's word
31 "Gnarly!"
34 School of the future?
35 "Stupid ___ stupid does"
36 Swear words?
37 ABACUS
42 Before, of yore
43 Noted Thai textile
44 Funnyman Philips
45 Symbol of industriousness
46 ___ Paese (semi-soft cheese)
47 Exploding "pineapple"
51 In the past
53 Classic Ferrari or Pontiac
55 Juniper drink
56 BE TOO EAGER
62 Any Muslim
63 Jarome of the Flames
64 Social reformer Jacob
65 Conk out
66 Ratted out
67 Animal egg containers
68 First word uttered after a birth
69 Cockeyed

DOWN

1 Wait ___ attitude
2 Cobbler container
3 Like a snug bug, maybe
4 It's this in Trois-Rivières
5 Henry VI founded it
6 ___ of Solomon
7 Professional grp.
8 Family feast entrée
9 Stage direction
10 Sought answers
11 Riot cause, sometimes
12 Dashiell Hammett dog
13 Type of phone book, for short
19 What a raised hand often means
21 Impatient, with "up"
26 Something up one's sleeve
27 Blows up
28 Creepy
30 *Politically Incorrect* host Bill
32 Blurbs
33 E, in Morse code
35 Squid's squirt
37 Caspian, for one
38 Mantel piece
39 Tinny-sounding
40 Ringing comment
41 Many, many moons
47 Moo ___ gai pan
48 Axe to grind, maybe
49 *Gunsmoke* marshal Matt
50 Child of Chibougamau
52 It's blown or cut
54 Nature's air conditioners
56 Christmas trees
57 Nepal's continent
58 Middle of Caesar's boast
59 Silent film star Naldi
60 They're sometimes bruised
61 Flowerpot site

38 *It's Neapolitan*

ACROSS

1 They're suckers, for short
5 Pull up to a bar?
9 Riga resident
13 Speller's words
14 Be laid up with
15 Cool and detached
17 Bosnia peacekeeping grp.
18 Answer man Trebek
19 Hizzoner
20 George's songwriting partner
21 Chat-room chuckle
22 Vocalist's vibration
24 Tavern sign
26 Season in the *soleil*
27 Tornadic Looney Tunes devil, for short
28 Property claims
29 Alternative flavour to 1-Down
32 Standout athletes
34 Out of bed
35 Pop quiz, for one
36 ___ & Span (household cleanser)
37 They carry stuff
40 Pete Rose got the most ever
44 Alternative flavour to 1-Down
46 '60s trendy jacket name
47 Scrape by, with "out"
48 Pooh's pal
49 When both hands are up
50 Martin Luther King's hometown
53 Six-pack makeup?
54 *Invasion of the Body Snatchers* container
55 "Lemon Tree" singer Lopez
56 Suggestive
58 Rap's Salt-N- ___
59 Site of the 1988 Summer Olympics
60 Gets it wrong
61 Palm-reader's start
62 Kitchen addition
63 Fiddle duet?
64 Neptune and Pluto, e.g.

DOWN

1 With 43-Down, malt-shop offerings
2 Skinny comparison
3 High point in Halifax
4 Cone head?
5 Bedlam
6 Place of mirrors
7 Elvis Presley's "___ Lost You"
8 Abutting
9 Pathetic
10 Jack of old oaters
11 Cars since 1935
12 Past the deadline
16 With 37-Down, theme of this puzzle
21 Mr. Pearson
23 Sportscast wrap-ups
25 Site for an arch
26 Canadian speech mannerisms
29 Computer screen: Abbr.
30 Adjusts to the surroundings
31 Leaf-like growth on rocks
33 Postulate
36 Utter
37 See 16-Down
38 Symbol of strength
39 "The Waste Land" poet
40 Pal in the 'hood
41 "That's my wish," in other words
42 Marched
43 See 1-Down
45 Had a belly laugh
49 Yawning chasm
51 "Sometimes you feel like ___ ..."
52 The longest river in the world
53 Field measure
57 "Is" in another form
58 Slob

39 Repeat After Me

ACROSS

1 Canada's secret agts.
5 "... say, and not ___"
10 In order (to)
14 One-time MLA, now political commentator Mair
15 Brief synopsis
16 Gillette razor brand
17 Irish New Age singer
18 Manhattan landmark, once
20 The Normandy Campaign was part of it: Abbr.
21 Tonic go-with
22 Adds to the payroll
23 Life insurance contract clause
28 Lennon's john
29 Figures of speech
30 Mark of disgrace
33 "Suzie Q" band, for short
34 Just misses, as a putt
38 Proverb about blame sharing, with "It"
41 Flies, to spiders
42 Calendar abbr.
43 They keep to themselves
44 BC footballers
46 Poetic tribute
47 Tournament card game with partners
54 Its mecca is Mecca
55 Grazing area
56 Word before and after "in"
57 Poker variation
61 Years abroad
62 Playing with a full deck
63 Nick of *Cape Fear*
64 Be laid up with
65 Sounds of disapproval
66 Simmering
67 Galoots

DOWN

1 Words to live by
2 ___ Domingo
3 Answer to "May I?"
4 Beaufort, for one
5 Bandleader Shaw
6 Like some coat linings
7 Here, for Henri
8 Karate level
9 Make a choice
10 Led through the foyer
11 Cheri of *Liar Liar*
12 Montréal street sign
13 Smart-mouthed
19 Resistance units
21 Grabs (onto)
24 One over in golf
25 Worthless: Var.
26 Red Green's tape type
27 Get on the list
30 Engine additive letters
31 Bad stuff in cigarettes
32 Room at the top?
34 "Amazing" magician
35 Yawner's self-diagnosis
36 Dept. head
37 ABBA tune
39 Horse's halter?
40 Start of an Irish lullaby
44 Margarita ingredient
45 Deal with
47 Accomplished, once
48 "___ directed"
49 Put (down), as money
50 Shoe-store stock
51 Moisten in the morn
52 Michael Jackson trademark
53 Someone ___ fault
58 Cone or Cat preceder
59 Took first
60 Green around the gills
61 Discovery cry

40 *I Said, Repeat After Me!*

ACROSS

1 *Chico and ___* ('70s sitcom)
7 City on BC's Fraser River
11 *Queen Mary* pronoun
14 First-aid liquid
15 Puts it on plastic
16 In a dither, with "up"
17 Reconsiders
19 Ottawa's National ___ Gallery
20 Realtor's parcel
21 LPs' better halves, often
22 "Why, ___ delighted!"
23 PetroCan rival
25 Rage
26 *The Naked Maja* artist
27 Film featuring Felix and Oscar
32 ___ work (begin a project)
35 Pizzeria fixture
36 Legal abbr.
37 Crosby or Como
40 Kind of diving
42 Dadaist Jean
43 Big times
45 Itsy bits
46 Bert and Nan or Flossie and Freddie
50 Vent verbally
51 Common Market inits.
52 "Oh, very funny!"
56 Funny-bone neighbour
57 Winged fisher
60 ___ Paese cheese
61 Beaufort, for one
62 "Pronto!"
64 US payroll datum
65 Entice
66 Harder on the eyes
67 Cape Town's ctry.
68 Grp. or org.
69 Glossy leather

DOWN

1 Novel start
2 Sounds from Santa
3 Readies to be read
4 Stovetop setting: Abbr.
5 "(You're) Having My Baby" singer
6 Ogopogo's Scottish cousin
7 "Fine" situation
8 Baby's boo-boo
9 Chest muscles: Abbr.
10 Suffix with Vietnam or Japan
11 Dubious background
12 Insomniac's drink
13 Novel ending
18 Greenhorn: Var.
22 Promise to pay
24 Sgt. Snorkel's dog
26 Entered
28 "Cross my heart!"
29 Movie rental
30 Middle key
31 Trudeau guesses: Abbr.
32 Striker's bane
33 Fault-free
34 Big cheese
38 Before, to Byron
39 Slice of light
41 Like a five-star hotel
44 King of horror
47 ___ Act (Constitution of 1867)
48 Are no longer
49 Needed defrosting
53 American activist Hoffman
54 Trojan beauty
55 At the ready
56 "Back in the ___" (Beatles)
57 Burden
58 Gibraltar and Magellan: Abbr.
59 Hindu means to inner peace
62 Suffix with pay
63 To the max

41 | *En-abled Puzzle*

ACROSS

1 Spud
6 Stable parent
10 Carpentry clamp
14 Prefix meaning "people"
15 Rock star, to teens
16 BC Lions' defensive stats
17 Americano lead-in
18 Not ideological, perhaps
20 Like a 911 call: Abbr.
21 Had it up to here
22 Raptors org.
23 Greek god of the forest
24 Scrub-brush target
25 Evaded
27 Kind of chart
30 Observed, to Tweety Bird
31 Political campaign tactic
32 Sounded like a pig
35 Foreigner's language, sometimes
39 Sung words
40 Early 1940s computer
42 ___-relief
45 Supped
46 DeCarlo of *The Munsters*
47 ___ Triomphe
50 Dander
51 Suffix with lemon or lime
52 Tranquility
56 "Don't look ___!"
57 List of places to go
58 It's a wrap
59 Egyptian Christian
60 Crafty move
61 What elms provide
62 Barflies
63 Leave in, to an editor
64 German steel city

DOWN

1 Length of a curling game, usually
2 Cold War worry
3 Sewing machine gizmo
4 ___'acte
5 School of the future?
6 Temptress of myth
7 French conception
8 Chestnut-coloured
9 High-fashion mag
10 Glare deterrent
11 Have a hunch
12 Mark of shame
13 Shun
19 Gerund finish
21 Long-faced
23 Bright-eyed and bushy-tailed
26 London lockup
27 Slangy gun
28 Bed and breakfast sites
29 Ticker tape, briefly?
32 "I'll get right ___"
33 Laval student
34 Flintstone's pet
36 Cenozoic or Paleozoic
37 Frank and his daughter Nancy
38 Manufactured without machines
41 Larry King's teevee station
42 ABCs
43 Playground retort
44 It has entrances and exits
46 No. of candles on a cake, e.g.
48 Results of parking lot mishaps
49 Ethyl ending
50 "The best ___ to come!"
53 Blows it
54 Astro or cosmo ending
55 Celtic language
56 Spa sounds
58 Dir. from Prince George to Kamloops

■ BARBARA OLSON

42 | *Auto Motives*

ACROSS

1 Bygone Fords
5 "Well, ___!" ("Aren't you sophisticated!")
11 Telly channel
14 Bubbly chocolate bar
15 Mythical hunk
16 Feel-good response
17 A couple of chatterboxes?
19 Ontario's 21st premier
20 Canary's comment
21 Eyes, poetically
22 French daily *Le* ___
23 Royal throne?
27 "I'll just be a jiff"
29 Ms. Marcos, and others
30 Meter leader
31 Utterly inane
34 Ship's helm and rudder?
39 Believe to be true
40 Obituary word
42 Joan of Arc's city
45 Subject to a tirade
48 Jim Morrison and bandsmen?
51 1984 Olympic skiing champ Phil
52 ___-Mart (place for pix)
53 "C'mon in!"
55 "It ___" (reply to "Who's there?")
56 Totally tanked?
60 Beatified ones: Abbr.
61 Poppins' parachute
62 Folk tail?
63 Atl. Canada shopper's add-on
64 "Maybe, maybe not"
65 ___ Helens

DOWN

1 Young fella
2 Of German origin
3 Come close
4 Progression from Pablum
5 Café au ___
6 Newspaper salesperson
7 Guitar played on the lap
8 ___ pinch
9 Verbal jab
10 Goofball
11 Prevented entry
12 Kids' cries
13 Treasure receptacles
18 Suit to ___
21 Canadian physician Sir William ___
22 Chic, in the '60s
24 Skid-row sights
25 Its relative major is G
26 Gen Xer's rock opera
28 It has lots of slots
32 Feeling, in Italy
33 "Ew, gross!"
35 In ___ (unborn)
36 "If __ it my way . . ."
37 Not a second early or late
38 Teen drivers
41 Season in the *soleil*
42 Stand-___ (aloof)
43 Fowl sleeping quarters
44 Medieval minstrel, perhaps
46 ". . . E-I-E-I-O, with ___ . . ."
47 Fire bomb jelly
49 Small brooks
50 Bob or bouffant
54 Roy Rogers' birth name
56 US agent's org.
57 Cursor's place, often
58 On-line titter
59 *Da Vinci's Inquest* fig.

43 | *Centre Pieces*

ACROSS

1 Is remorseful
5 Cardiologists' concerns
11 Q-U separator
14 Env. addition
15 Circus attractions of old
16 It starts *le 21 juin*, usually
17 Lizard look-alikes
19 Rummy player's cry
20 Country's Tritt
21 "...rose ___ rose..."
   (Gertrude Stein)
22 Clumsy clods
23 Lord Black's wife
24 Take apart
26 Balcony
28 Champagne classes?
29 Broadbent and Mirvish
30 Nah's opposite
33 History
34 Business go-between,
   and a clue to this puzzle's
   theme
37 Comparable to a hatter
40 Ham in a can
41 Brief thank-yous
44 Offers around
46 Downsize, maybe

49 Long-lasting wave
52 ___-Potti (camper's biffy)
53 Towel inscription
54 Menu phrase
55 Hit close to home
56 Legend ending
57 Tanzanian peak
59 Moon mobile: Abbr.
60 John's co-star in *Grease*
61 Neighbour of Wash.
62 Three in Torino
63 Evaluate
64 Pansy pads

DOWN

1 Say again
2 Lacking heat?
3 Iced treats
4 Drool
5 *Law & Order* figs.
6 "Get your ___!" (greedy
   comment)
7 Ulnae neighbours
8 Long braid
9 Chalet, often
10 Deflating sound
11 Yachting event
12 Zips it

13 Most anxious
18 Brian's wife or Ben's
   mom
22 Something to cry over
24 Adam Sandler's *Mr. ___*
25 Jasper's prov.
27 Dancer Charisse
31 Heidi's hangout
32 Soul mate
34 School mistresses, once
35 Comics light bulb
36 Mrs. in Mascouche
37 Pavement component
38 Less opaque
39 Engaging words?
41 It's very rare on a menu
42 Let out, in a way
43 Ancient mariners
45 Some homebodies?
47 Emulated Rumpelstiltskin
48 Swindler's work
50 Island off Manhattan
51 Wet behind the ears
55 Lamb's laments
57 Popular campground
   initials
58 Wrong start

44 | *A Likely Story*

ACROSS

1 Something passed along
7 OPEC units
11 Snapshot
14 In ___ (somewhat)
15 Typical west-coast attire
17 Where it's going while ripening
18 Montréal CFLer
19 Indulging in deception
21 Hurt severely
23 "Right on!"
24 ___ for tat
25 Glaciers, mostly
26 Not "agin"
27 Ammunition
31 Raw-fish dish
33 Birling competition
34 Indulging in deception
38 Contestants' ranks
39 Character builders?
42 They're marked with yellow
45 "I am such a dope!"
47 Corrida cheer
48 Wanted-poster letters
49 Alternatives
50 Cyberspeak opinion lead-in: Abbr.
51 Indulging in deception

57 Vampire's fang, e.g.
58 One-dimensional
61 Camper's need
62 Its pH is higher than 7
63 Has too much, for short
64 Get an ___ effort
65 Idle chatter, often

DOWN

1 Fink
2 *For the Boys* subj.
3 Most untidy
4 Two bells, at sea
5 Computer jockey
6 Late-night flight, slangily
7 Small nails
8 Island east of Java
9 BC CFLer
10 Tightly tucked in
11 Tiny in Trois-Rivières
12 Response to "Where's the last piece of cake?"
13 Wave tops
16 Hair goop
20 ___ Lingus (Irish carrier)
21 Start to take
22 Start to puncture
26 Manicurist, at times
27 Site for a cranberry crop

28 Now-retired NHL badboy Samuelsson
29 Janet of "Psycho"
30 Ear or brain part
32 "___ real nowhere man" (Beatles lyric)
33 IV league?
35 Went first
36 Doorman's requests
37 Stir-fry veggies
40 Whitney or Wallach
41 Baste or gather
42 Regained consciousness
43 Gave the go-ahead
44 Regains consciousness
45 Joanne of *Abie's Irish Rose*
46 Banner seen at the Canada Cup
49 Survey category
50 Dark moods
52 Addams Family cousin
53 "Fat chance"
54 Flub
55 July 1944 attack site
56 Thin pastry for spanakopita
59 Poet of pugilism
60 Dead letters?

■ DAVE MACLEOD

45 Unhatched Chickens

ACROSS

1 Use plastic at the store
7 Upper limit, in ads
10 Roulette bet
13 Some street people
14 Bit of reality?
15 "Listen up!"
16 Lagoon enclosures
17 Pizzeria order
19 Part I of a lament about things never done
20 Guy Fawkes Day mo.
21 Pie in the sky?
22 Austrian river to the Danube
23 Uno + due
24 Earth or apple centre
26 Tapes over again
29 Kind of sin
31 It's not me in France
33 Strap marks
34 Letter before omega
37 Lament, part II
39 ___ Haw (old country music show)
40 Pretend to be
42 Father and son Indy 500 winners
44 Bouncer's selection, often
46 Coat ___ (family insignia)
50 Side squared, for squares
51 Hero of The Matrix
52 On a ___ (partying)
53 Have a bawl
54 Greyhound stop: Abbr.
55 Lament, part III
57 Books of synonyms
59 Turn off, in a way
60 The Chiffons' "___ So Fine"
61 I smell ___
62 Canadiens star
63 Spanish gold
64 With it, '50s-style
65 Charity recipients

DOWN

1 One with a plug in his mouth
2 Knee-slapper
3 Be plentiful
4 Gets ready to ship, as a carpet
5 Neuter at the farm
6 What she is in Italy
7 Some magnetic trains
8 Letter ender
9 Strikes (out)
10 With 36-Down, lament continued
11 Finish, as a cake
12 Egg covering in spring
14 Puzzle's words of advice for avoiding disappointment
18 Desi's daughter
25 Other than this
27 Many opera villains
28 Sibilant silencer
30 The Lord of the Rings figure
32 Place for cheese
34 Normal or legal prefix
35 Really hot day
36 End of lament
38 God: Lat.
41 "All in ___ work"
43 Occupied, as a saddle
45 Make certain
47 Baseball Hall-of-Fame pitcher Fingers
48 Electronic component
49 Rocket parts
55 Signalled an actor
56 Clued in about
57 However, for short
58 Reaction to a back rub, maybe

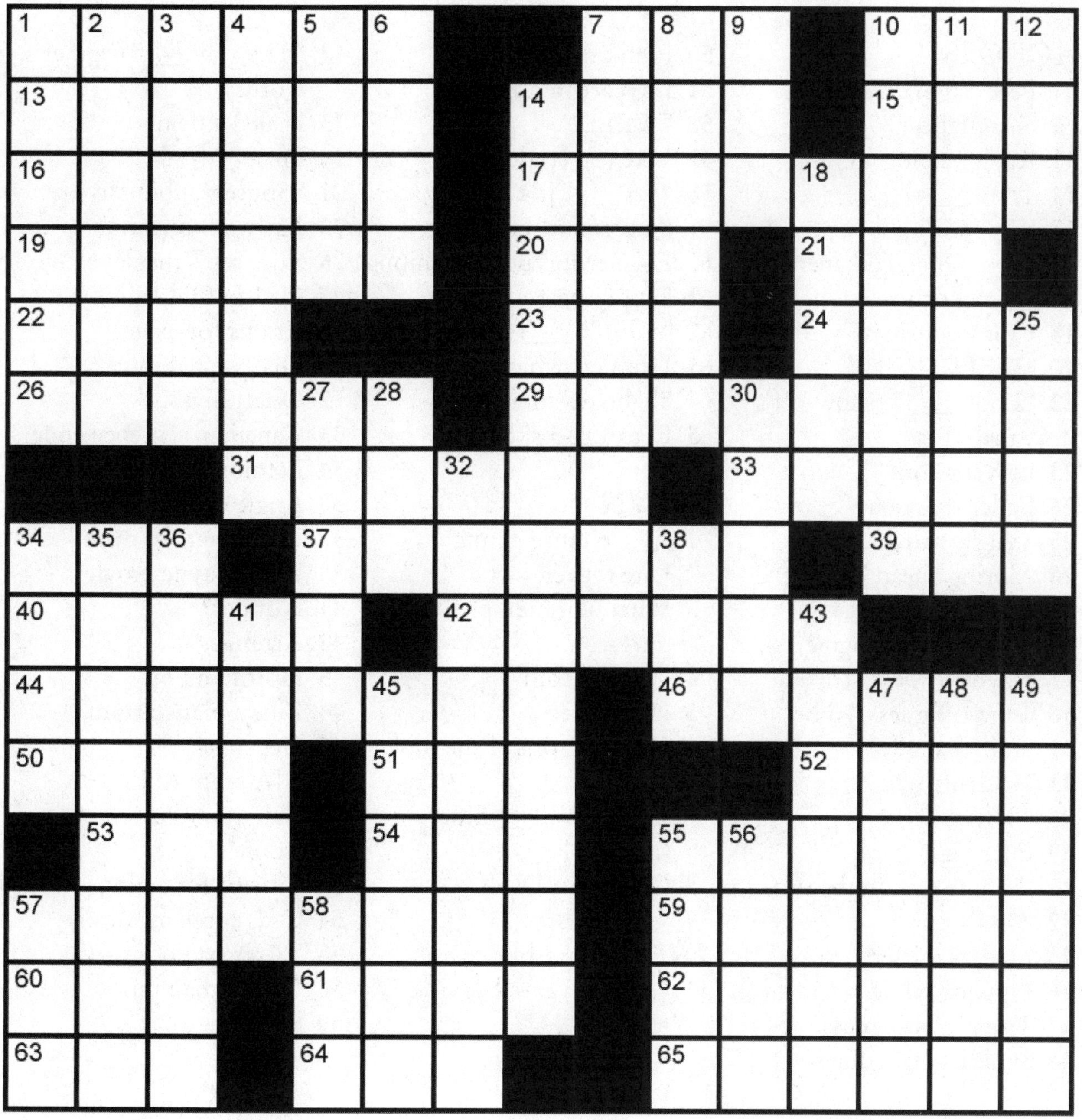

46 Well, Well, Well

ACROSS

1 Peruvian natives
6 Sheer fabric
11 Karaoke plug-in
14 Terra ___
15 Wrapped up
16 Early Oiler Tikkanen
17 ___ majority
18 Fails in business
20 "WELL?"
22 "Look ___!" (show-off's words)
23 Latvia's cont.
24 Ballerina's bend
25 Shaggy hairdo
26 "Spring ahead" setting: Abbr.
27 CEO's wall hanging, maybe
30 Take-off guess: Abbr.
31 Stole, slangily
33 No-frills
35 "WELL, . . ."
39 Flies high
40 Became one on the run
42 Family gal
45 Madras mister
46 Opp. of NNW
47 Tire pressure meas.
48 Superlative endings
50 Prefix meaning "needle"
51 Daycare denizens
52 "WELL!"
57 Like top students
58 "It's ___ , it's . . ." (*Superman* refrain)
60 Former Egypt-Syr. union
61 Supply new weapons
62 "I don't ___ respect"
63 Use a crowbar
64 Slight advantages
65 Retort to a skeptic

DOWN

1 "___ picture paints . . ."
2 Late retirer
3 What Chrétien met face on?
4 "Get ___ on!"
5 Home free
6 Chill in front of the tube, say
7 "With God ___ Side" (Bob Dylan)
8 Checked a DOB
9 ___-majesté
10 The 3 Rs: Abbr.
11 Give unwanted advice, maybe
12 "The way ___" (opiner's words)
13 Issued a ticket
19 Furtive drink
21 Spouse's submissive reply
22 Early abbreviations
26 Sales rep's displays
27 1101 in Old Rome
28 Crams for exams
29 Oft-twisted joint
32 Quart divs.
33 Canadian sentence enders
34 Lennon's love
36 Angle opener
37 Like dawn, to dusk
38 John Wayne movies
41 Not dat?
42 Arranges
43 Hoffman flop
44 Like a planetarium
46 Gets lost
49 VIA stop: Abbr.
50 Other, in Outremont
51 Rome's river
53 Title fit for a king
54 Old, euphemistically
55 '70s broadloom style
56 East-Indian music
59 Scooby-___

47 | *Epitaph*

ACROSS

1 Have trouble with siblings?
5 Mote
10 Mizzen, e.g.
14 *The Thin Man* terrier
15 2002 Oscar winner Berry
16 Combining form for "within"
17 One looking ahead, maybe
18 Step-up
20 START OF AN EPITAPH
22 Measure of evidence
23 Really bothered
24 Works in the States
27 One of the McGarrigle sisters
29 Small egg
30 Refuse
32 Drug amount
36 Wilfrid Laurier title
37 MIDDLE OF EPITAPH
40 Bake sale org.
41 ___ St. Vincent Millay
43 Formerly, formerly
44 Dog bane
46 Study at the last minute
48 Kind of hammer
49 Iraqi port
52 Expression of disbelief
54 END OF EPITAPH
60 Hillbilly's liquor store
61 Hockey's Mikita
62 Like Twiggy
63 Edit text
64 Sicilian spouter
65 Plant support
66 Fords, as a stream
67 *Days of Our Lives*, for one

DOWN

1 Punishment for a tar, maybe
2 Comment after the fog clears
3 Fret
4 Sun shield
5 Bush trimmers
6 Old hat
7 Heston role (1961)
8 Epitome of happiness
9 Beach detritus
10 Measured, as electricity
11 Inner self
12 Brown ermine
13 1,000 kilograms
19 Got down
21 Vixen
24 Misplace
25 Eager
26 Set afire
27 Mend, as bone
28 Gob's yes
30 Campus residence, commonly
31 Both Begleys
33 Newspaper page, for short
34 Males-only party
35 Abate
38 "Isn't ___ bit like you and me?" (Beatles lyric)
39 Key above C
42 CSIS, e.g.
45 Jerry and Jerry Lee
47 Ewe's beaus
48 Pottery pieces
49 Fails at the box office
50 Under way
51 Quick bread
52 Ached
53 Play setting
55 Expression of relief
56 Succotash bean
57 Sgt. Snorkel's dog
58 *Peter Pan* pooch
59 Ginger cookie

■ BARBARA OLSON

48 | *Tell Me the News*

ACROSS

1 Hiker's stuff
5 Necklace fastener
10 Mrs. Mulroney
14 Fido's food
15 Down in the mouth
16 "Don't have ___!"
17 Real humdinger
19 Dos and don'ts, for short
20 Mail for Mansbridge and crew, with *The*?
22 "The stage ___"
23 Fleur-de-___
24 BC's Okanagan output
28 Day of rest: Abbr.
30 Low-cost food brand
31 Resident of the nation's capital
35 Grp. seen in huddles
37 Commandment word
38 "... him exclaim, ___ he drove ..."
39 Royal messenger in Cow Town?
44 ___ new course
45 ___ crash course
46 Guesstimator's opener
47 PC's upper-left key
50 Hockey analyst Harry

54 Early riser in a BC city?
57 Sighed words
60 *Canadian Idol* singer, for one
61 "Hogwash!"
62 Being broadcast
63 Civil grad: Abbr.
64 Get fixed, in a way
65 After a fashion, lazily
66 Manuscript encl.

DOWN

1 Bouquet ___ (herb bundle)
2 Sewing-machine inventor Howe
3 GP's bookings
4 Most up
5 "Follow me," quickly
6 Concerning folk knowledge
7 In a fitting way
8 Is oozy
9 Firebug, for short
10 Olive's place
11 Finish the cake
12 Use a yarder and choker
13 Sounds of dismay
18 "___ all" ("No trouble")

21 Lassie, for one
25 Seeing stars
26 Part of ER: Abbr.
27 Lévesque of Québec
29 Iraq's second-largest city
30 Prefix with -glycerin
31 Spanish stews
32 Word of wonder
33 Spa utterance
34 Key for Débussy
35 301 in Old Rome
36 Saudi Arabian king until 2005
40 In a sombre way
41 "Back ___" ("Ditto")
42 Murray and McLellan
43 Ophelia's brother
47 No-frills
48 Sub's guide
49 "___ out!"
51 Yoga position
52 Breathers?
53 Between, in Baie-Comeau
55 Cpls. and others
56 Aloe ___
57 Place for a six-pack at the gym
58 Eskimo word
59 Prov. riding rep.

49 Northern Heroes

ACROSS

1 Awkward conversation fillers
4 Bad time for Caesar
8 Easy-to-swallow pill
14 Pudgy
16 Fascination
17 Creative planner
18 Laughed loudly
19 1970s comic book superhero
21 Feed the kitty
22 Go in to the ankles
23 Flood protection
28 ___ d'Or Lake, Cape Breton
32 Police dept. alert
35 "___ on first?" (Costello)
36 Lettuce or cabbage
37 1950s TV hero "of the Yukon"
41 Fake name
42 They're caught on the beach
43 Cry of mock fright
44 Cribbage markers
45 Be rude with, in a way
48 Big name in copiers
50 "___ silly question ..."
54 21st century weekly CTV heroes?
59 Voicing disapproval
61 Sault ___, ON
62 One in Canada, commonly
63 Oil, slangily
64 Doesn't rest easy
65 Complete collections
66 CSIS employee

DOWN

1 Author Jong
2 Pterodactyl over Tokyo
3 Caught some Zs
4 *Res ___ loquitur* (legal phrase)
5 Tie of the Leafs
6 Grand style
7 Harmony, briefly
8 ___ *Knowledge*: 1971 Nicholson film
9 So all can hear
10 Pills that do nothing?
11 Skulk
12 Before, of yore
13 Hockey Hall of Famer Lindsay
15 Eastwood's *Rawhide* role
20 Leatherworker's tool
24 Meadow mamas
25 Discovery cry
26 Took first
27 Latin stars
29 Mechanical learning method
30 Lotion ingredient
31 Went under
32 Quickly, quickly
33 Brazilian soccer great
34 Punishment for a sailor, maybe
36 Tableland
38 Carriers under city streets
39 Duffer's goal
40 Reuben bread
45 Rocket parts
46 Small fry
47 Fanfares
49 Deep subject for navel gazers?
51 A bit, colloquially
52 Film-set light
53 "Take ___" (host's request)
54 Sounds like a pigeon
55 Believers' suffixes
56 Suit to ___
57 Call in a crowded bakery
58 "___ helpless as a kitten ..."
59 Deli order
60 Hugs, on paper

■ BARBARA OLSON

50 | *Members of the Club*

ACROSS

1 College VIP, so he thinks
5 Third Greek letter
10 Down Under how do
14 Sitarist Shankar
15 Kodiak native
16 Saturn or Mercury
17 Taskbar item
18 Speak frankly
20 Canadian-born talk show host Alan
22 Robert of *The Sopranos*
23 Goth's gloomier cousin
24 "Same here"
25 Seismic wave
27 Reversible fabric
29 Dark times, briefly
32 "Rule, Britannia" composer
35 When to pick up?: Abbr.
36 Watchmaker
37 Rent splitters
39 Imams' temples
40 Actor John of *Serendipity*
41 "Give ___ break!"
42 American alternative magazine
43 Kind of daisy
44 Nodder's comment
46 Tenor Plácido

48 "Wait ___!" (Austin Powers' line)
52 Inflation abbr.
54 Roman years
55 Like some patches
56 *Murder in the First* star
59 Sphere starter
60 St. Paul's Cathedral architect
61 Cyber-commerce
62 Wash the deck
63 "Blah blah blah," when repeated
64 Perry Mason's secretary
65 Ring ___ (kid's game)

DOWN

1 Canucks' cousins
2 Village People title adjective
3 Egg-shaped
4 Mexican spring celebration
5 Crowd stopper
6 King runner-up?
7 Singer Etheridge
8 Tootoosis' tootsy warmer
9 When to watch Peter Mansbridge
10 Long-jawed fish

11 Do battle
12 "Up and ___!"
13 It has its ups and downs
19 The "tilted" planet
21 Spectra maker
25 Makes lace
26 Spineless person
28 26-Down descriptor
30 Like four and twenty
31 Ed.'s receipt
32 With the bow, in music
33 Béchemal basis
34 Headed south in a hurry
36 Wild swine
38 He had a cool delivery
39 "Let ___!"
41 Sprinkled with stardust, maybe
44 Coming naturally
45 Hammer and anvil locale
47 Sick at home
49 Split ___ (bisect)
50 Deep sleeps
51 Protuberances
52 Tree-lined road: Abbr.
53 Doris Day refrain
55 Where a King might play
57 "___ pig's eye!"
58 Sea slick

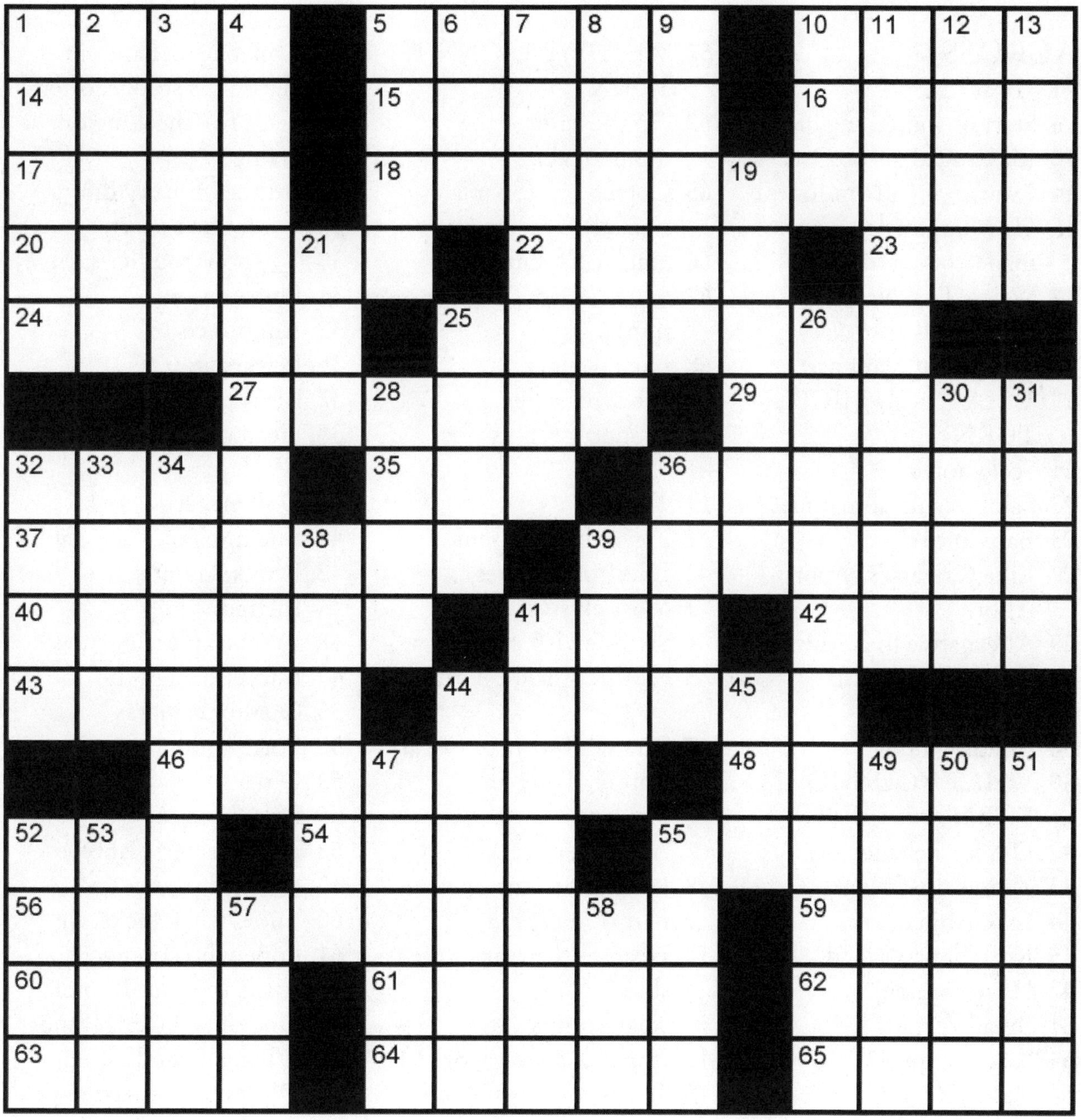

51 Taking Turns

ACROSS

1 "Beat it!"
6 Start of something big?
10 It's exuded at the Oscars
14 "She's ___" (Tom Jones)
15 How large sales are often made
17 Where Exodus may be found
18 Absorbent plant parts
19 WHAT YOU MIGHT TURN
21 Scale notes
22 Salon result, sometimes
23 Baby bird?
27 Like Calgary's airport: Abbr.
29 Alternative to a Segway
33 Run out of steam
34 Before, of yore
36 Building up
39 WHAT YOU SHOULD TURN
42 D+, for instance
43 Tennis do-over
44 Like Abner
45 Kofi Annan's land
47 Have coming
51 Bread spreads
54 "... ___ quit!"
56 Yes to Yoshihito
57 WHAT YOU CAN'T TURN
62 On the spur of the moment (Lat.)
65 Correo ___ (Spanish airmail)
66 Smell of a semi
67 ___ It (1983 Tom Cruise film)
68 Dine partner
69 What pigs dig
70 Property claims

DOWN

1 Zen enlightenment
2 Like goat hooves
3 Most elusive
4 Sixth Jewish month
5 "If that's true I'll eat ___!"
6 Rita who won an Oscar, Emmy, Tony and Grammy
7 Aplenty, once
8 London lockup
9 Part of un opéra
10 Head to the rear of the ship
11 That homme
12 It makes a wok work?
13 The Kootenays: Abbr.
16 Princely name, in brief
20 Convention handout
24 Garfield's stooge, often
25 Place for checking or saving
26 Source of many drafts
28 Look like a satyr
30 ___-boo (toddler's game)
31 Flub
32 Announce
35 Letters after CD
37 Revolutionary Guevara
38 Head of Haiti?
39 Work hard
40 Golf target
41 Buckingham Palace abbr.
42 It was Arafat's grp.
46 Ineffectual
48 "You can lead ___ ..."
49 Burst through the door
50 Quality cameras
52 Portly plus
53 Ditto
55 Poker notice
58 Two-stripers: Abbr.
59 ___-Aid
60 The Dixie Chicks, e.g.
61 Pope who convinced Attila to spare Rome
62 One of eight Eng. kings
63 When all hands are up?
64 Olympic gymnastics goal

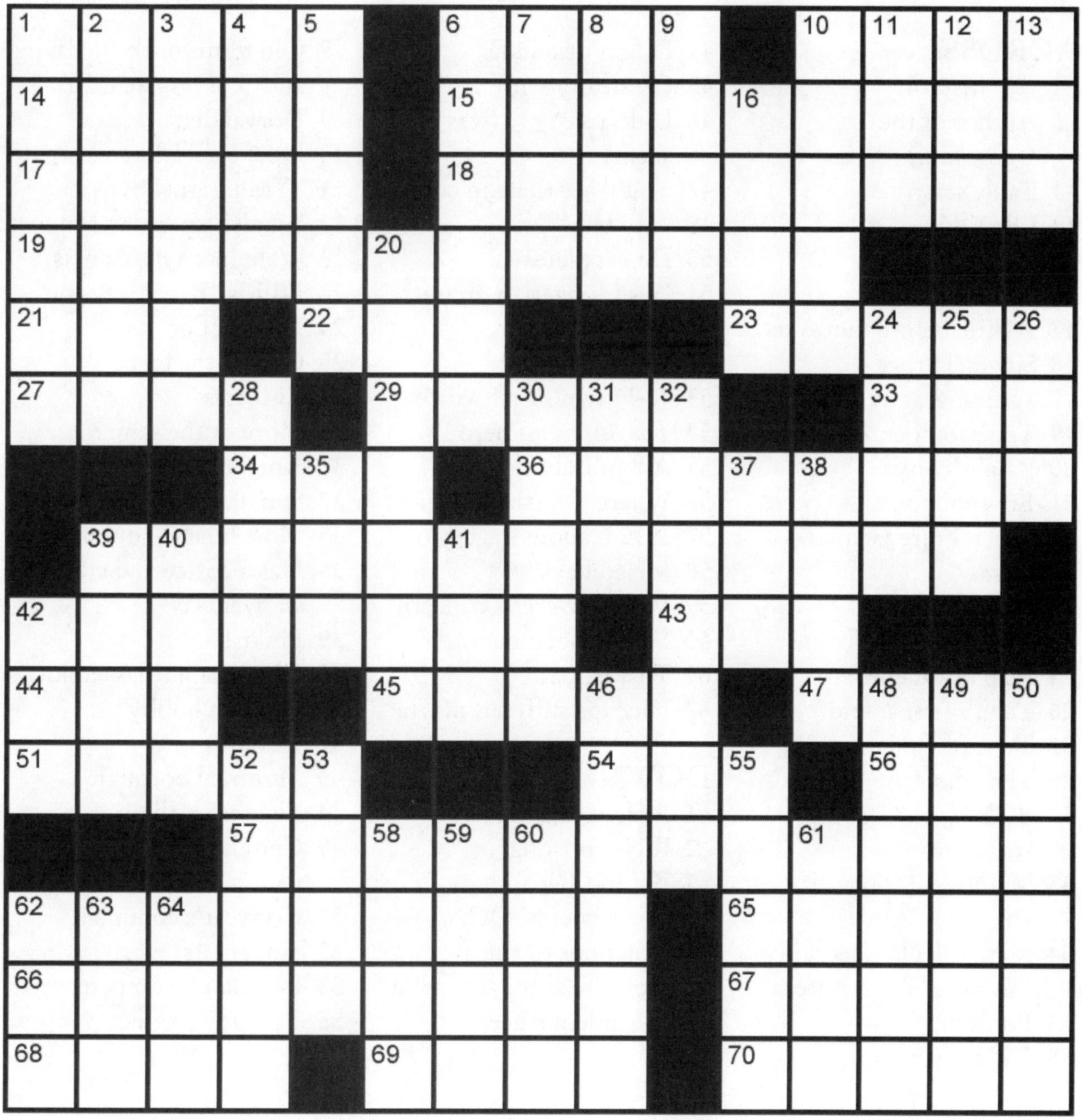

52 *Grey Areas in Math*

ACROSS

1 ___-Bismol
6 Author of the *Goosebumps* series
11 Table scrap
14 Old Olds
15 Praise
16 Half of a sob
17 A little before the hour
18 Singer Turner's autobiography
19 Transatl. flier, once
20 Rajahs' wives
21 Low sounds?
22 When Frère Jacques sleeps
23 Much lead-in
24 It's left on the ocean
25 Map of Québec?
26 Tuba's first sound
27 Type of bank acct.
28 The whole ___
30 BC's Myra Canyon structures
33 Mauna ___ (Hawaiian volcano)
34 Math calculations, and this puzzle's grey areas
37 Pop's bro
38 Didn't have enough

41 Doesn't exclude
45 Go steady with
46 Didn't say ___ (was silent)
47 You'll see them in court
48 "My bad!"
50 Desert plateau
51 '50s Hungarian premier Nagy
52 Start to choke?
53 40-Down's first word
54 *The Simpsons* nerd
55 All, in Italy
56 Where ___ (the hot spot)
57 1990 Capote stage-bio
58 Mixed bags
59 Mail deliverer's concern
60 Lamp attachment?
61 That is: Lat.
62 Hiccups sufferer, maybe

DOWN

1 Ardent flag-waver
2 Rigby of song
3 Bic and Berol?
4 ___-Rivières, QC.
5 Reactions to slugs
6 Don't read the fine print
7 D-student's need

8 Old term for those having an IQ of less than 20
9 Dorval denials
10 Hockey's Tikkanen
11 "Yeah, right"
12 Spanish-speaking Muppet
13 Walk like a 62-Across
22 NFL's "Broadway Joe"
24 Dive's opposite
25 Get off the fence
27 Evel acts
29 More of the same?
31 Knight-to-be
32 Sun. talk
35 Most hoarse-sounding
36 Has a coffee and cold shower, say
39 Pinkish
40 Champagne glass holder
41 Has as a hobby
42 Uno, for one
43 Montréal borough
44 Fighter jet flight
49 Certain palindromic names
50 Copycat's comment
52 January 1st word
53 Dixieland trumpeter Al
55 You, to Yvonne

53 | *Pucker Up*

ACROSS

1 Is loose-lipped
6 "___ each life a little rain . . ."
10 Matador's red cloak
14 Wrecker's haul, maybe
15 Former queen of Jordan
16 Mishmash
17 Walkerton water worry
18 Like someone told to forget it
20 Start of a Groucho Marx quip
22 Seminary subj.
23 Snowmobiles, informally
24 Dead Sea find in 1947
28 Most quickly
32 Central Swiss district
33 Erode, with "into"
35 Took off for
36 More of Marx's quip
41 Tip over
42 Prov. whose flower is the white trillium
43 Calgary's commuter train syst.
44 Small change in Spain, once
47 Casually breezes by
50 ___ living (make ends meet)
52 ___ Jima (WW II battle site)
53 End of Marx's quip
59 Hotly debated topic
60 ". . . ring, ___ wed"
61 Certain palindrome opener
62 American Sioux
63 Dressed to the ___
64 Breathing-related: Abbr.
65 ___ buco
66 Have on

DOWN

1 Botched (it)
2 First name in Solidarity
3 ". . . cow, E-I-E-I-O, with ___ . . ."
4 Theme music from *10*
5 Blubber
6 "Are you ___ out?"
7 They may be proper
8 Comes to
9 Part of a plaint by Juliet
10 Frigid spell
11 His: Fr.
12 Early Brit
13 Just dandy
19 Bogart topper
21 Ms. DeGeneres
24 Farmer's alarm
25 It's flatter than a pancake
26 Jasmine and basmati
27 Hang loose
29 ___ Gay (WW II plane)
30 Raconteur's offering
31 Wrongdoings at the bar
34 A couple
37 Wading, say
38 Pooches' pendants
39 Some articles
40 Result of an oil spill?
45 "Am not!" retort
46 Nose-in-the-air types
48 Young suitors
49 Lead that should be followed
51 Frizzy dos
53 Agree
54 WWW addresses
55 "I ___ mad!"
56 Fretter's cry
57 Dutch painter Jan van der ___
58 Sat., to Sun.
59 Wide partner

54 *Menacing Puzzle*

ACROSS

1 Like ABCs
6 Dang!
10 Where you live, casually
14 ___ cologne
15 *The Time Machine* people
16 Frequently
17 Menacing substance for Superman
20 Composed
21 How to win in hockey
22 Big TV maker
25 Old ally of Fidel
26 Menacing evil genius from China
31 Nightwear, briefly
34 Enter stealthily
35 Swing around a pole
36 Castle or whistle feature
37 Probably
40 "Yeah, right"
41 The Duke of jazz
43 It went about 2,100 kph
44 Menacing cyborg from the future, with "The"
46 Employee ID
47 "___ won't!" (firm refusal)
48 Many newspaper ads
52 Take tiny bites
58 Menacing vegetation for Charlie Brown
61 Kept from swelling
62 Ingrid's *Casablanca* role
63 Beachy region
64 Moist in the morn
65 Good earth
66 Words before on or forth

DOWN

1 Does a doggie trick
2 Switzerland's longest river
3 Took to court
4 Piece of mind
5 It carries maple leaves on its back
6 Part of HRH
7 TV Tarzan Ron
8 Nightclub in a Manilow tune
9 Tacky display
10 He takes you on a tour through hell
11 "Would ___?"
12 "___ light?" (smoker's request)
13 Stern's opposite
18 TV host who's a frog
19 Pearl Harbor locale
23 Easy gallop
24 Cookout crasher
26 Little bits
27 Rent out again
28 Pedal pushers
29 "___ at 'em!"
30 "Gangsta's Paradise" rapper
31 Student of Socrates
32 One of your peers, perhaps
33 Caught in the act
34 Gomery Inquiry spy grp.
35 An army NCO
38 Part of a night out, likely
39 Modern ID
42 Pre-O trio
44 Swing on a rope
45 Involve
46 Like a flophouse
48 "___ you not!"
49 Good-natured
50 Do a slow burn
51 Normandy battle town
53 Words before boy or girl
54 Muffin stuff
55 Relax, as rules
56 Watch illuminators: Abbr.
57 PetroCan rival
59 "This ___ test"
60 *Platoon* setting

55 Dollars and Cents

ACROSS

1 ___ Québécois
6 Buying and selling
14 Actor Hawke
15 Shook hands, perhaps
16 Cheers (for)
17 Ancient, like Methuselah
18 With 53-Across, reality of 6-Across
20 Source of drafts
21 Caterer's heater
22 ___ of the valley
23 Web address ending
25 You, long ago
28 Flin ___, Manitoba
32 Having little time to waste
37 Rule for 6- and 63-Across
39 Member of Trail, BC's 1939 World Champ hockey team
40 It's sold in bars
41 Ural River city
42 Bad-mouth
44 Ceramics oven
47 Texas city on the Rio Grande
52 Is for more than one?
53 See 18-Across

58 Transient women
60 Below-average grade
61 Wind player's purchases
62 Cheri of *Liar Liar*
63 Buying and selling
64 Scottish wasteland shrub

DOWN

1 Salon jobs
2 On ___ (carousing)
3 River to Lake Geneva
4 Spud
5 Well-harmonized
6 Yarborough of NASCAR
7 Vegas quote
8 Have in mind
9 Mizzen, e.g.
10 Montréal summer hrs.
11 Form of therapeutic touch
12 "Ship of the desert"
13 Plaintive poem
15 Word heard in a herd
19 "Listen to the Music" band, familiarly
22 Toronto hockey dynasty
24 Elevator tunes
25 Used a keyboard

26 *The Adventures of Ozzie and* ___
27 "___ Beso" (Anka hit)
28 Bands on the radio
29 Skedaddle
30 Bouillon brand
31 Maker of top-end cameras
33 Harden, as plaster
34 A short life's story
35 Greek H
36 Second sight, briefly
38 Sea, to Marie
43 Sneaky feller
44 Barbecue treat
45 Ex-Yankee pitcher Hideki
46 Kid's blocks
48 ___-Bismol
49 To go on rue Ste-Catherine
50 Insulting remarks
51 Late actor Davis of *Do the Right Thing*
53 Small mountain lake
54 Chick follower?
55 Prevaricates
56 Sneakers brand
57 Mag. copy
59 Maui memento

56 Spin Cycle

ACROSS

1 Actor in chains
4 Canadian winter boot brand
9 "Be ___ and fix me some tea, please."
14 Gross!
15 With 36-Across and 63-Across, Beatles song for this puzzle
16 Slight colouration
17 "It's anybody's guess."
19 Blues guitarist Sleepy John ___
20 Like doilies
21 It may bring down the house
23 "Me too!"
26 Behind the line in hockey
27 "Want me to?"
28 Cry of facetious innocence
30 Lassie's beau
31 Update machinery
32 ___ once (suddenly)
35 Clubs: Abbr.
36 See 15-Across
37 Hi-fi sound?
41 Cosmetics name
43 Strand, or brownish-red
44 Spanish bear

47 Emerson's "jealous mistress"
48 Violates the rules
49 Coolio is one
52 Rite sites
53 Dangerous ocean swirl
56 Club costs
58 Ho Chi Minh's capital
59 Cold War fears
62 "Give it ___!"
63 See 15-Across
64 Something to shoot for
65 Refinement
66 Godzilla stomped it
67 Network: Abbr.

DOWN

1 Act like a baby
2 Works over
3 Recommended paint treatment
4 RR stop: Abbr.
5 Part of BYOB
6 Hindu sage
7 Biblical twin
8 Intergalactic dist.
9 Ordered out?
10 Brake components
11 Require
12 Motivation that may be hidden
13 Do some lawn repair

18 Huge circular storm
22 Churn up
24 Thrown for ___
25 Not even one
27 Madrid Mme.
28 "Luncheon on the Grass" painter
29 Like a relic
33 As ___ resort
34 Devastating wind
36 Ireland's ___ Lingus
38 Suitless declaration
39 Labrador airbase
40 Publicity, in slang
42 Infield cover
43 Wire measure
44 "... and the alternative is?"
45 Most of Mali
46 Voices
50 German toast: Var.
51 Chosen few
52 Have ___ (inspect)
54 Kiln for drying hops
55 First Holy Roman emperor
57 Belarus and Ukraine, once: Abbr.
60 "¡___ bien!"
61 "Takin' Care of Business" band

■ BARBARA OLSON

57 | *Disney Movies You Missed*

ACROSS

1 Verbal yawn
6 "It's a ___" ("Done")
10 Brood (over)
14 Cat-___-tails
15 Dance done in a grass skirt
16 Brazilian soccer great
17 Disney suspense set in Never Never Land?
19 Liberal Bob and family
20 Old French coin
21 Inspector Clouseau's roommate
22 Islamic holy city
23 Disney X-rated movie about a voyeuristic princess?
27 Agassi's wife
28 Grocery chain
29 Place for a maple leaf
32 Greek peak
33 It may be dense
36 Disney biography on a wealthy businessman and his ex-wife?
41 Like this clue's number
42 Pigeon calls
43 Mrs. Einstein
44 Be a fink
46 Tear apart
49 Disney comedy of errors?

53 There's a moral to his stories
54 Peek or bug ending
55 Kimono sash
58 "Qué ___?"
59 Disney "gangsta" movie?
62 It comes before "after," in fairly tales
63 Doesn't have ___ cent
64 Edmonton CFLer, for short
65 Funny Foxx
66 Country saloon door sign
67 *Chatelaine* focus

DOWN

1 Molson stock
2 ___'clock (1300 hours)
3 Ask for money, slangily
4 The loneliest *numéro*
5 He was *Talking to Americans*
6 Wistful question
7 Babble at length
8 Self-proclaimed "greatest"
9 School bake sale grp.
10 Bounteous meal
11 Serving of Red Rose, say
12 Send to the House
13 *Every Time ___ Goodbye* (Tom Hanks film, 1986)

18 Hemingway's nickname
22 ___ Work
24 Like nog or custard
25 Deep cut
26 CFB part
29 Andy Capp's wife
30 Wee tyke
31 Spoke to
32 Sudden-death spans: Abbr.
34 Meditative moans
35 Univ. student's bottom line
37 Start to ache, say
38 High time?
39 Chime part
40 Makeover
45 On deck
46 Tries again on eBay
47 Coal-black
48 Hangman's neckties?
49 Gradually ease (off)
50 Lift with effort
51 Shirt-size spot
52 Nutty as a fruitcake
56 Get frothy
57 Brossard brainchild
59 Dipstick wipe
60 "... man ___ mouse?"
61 Blended levy in Atl. Canada

1	2	3	4	5	■	6	7	8	9	■	10	11	12	13
14					■	15				■	16			
17				18				■		■	19			
20			■	21				■	■	22				
■	■	23	24				25	26						
■	■	■	27			■	28					■	■	■
29	30	31		■	■	■	32				■	33	34	35
36				37	38	39				40			
41			■	42				■	■	■	43			
■	■	44	45				■	46	47	48		■	■	■
49	50					51					52	■	■
53					■	54				■	55	56	57
58				■	59	60				61			
62				■	63				■	64				
65				■	66			■	67				

58 Making the Cut

ACROSS

1 Seductress
5 ___’ Pea
9 Bowlers’ hangouts
14 Winglike structures
15 Minor constellation?
16 Newsy bits
17 Massage targets
19 Actor Kline
20 Finish up a coif, at the salon
22 Back from the briny
23 Opp.
24 Mat. ward docs
25 Bend at the barre
27 SSE or NNW
30 *Falling Up* writer Silverstein
33 Bibliophile’s love
34 Prefix with form
35 Whisk snippings from shoulders, at the salon
39 Word with up or off
40 Canadian Timothy of the department store
41 Starting from
42 Discount ticket holders: Abbr.
43 Ariz. neighbour
44 Scale syllables
46 *Aladdin* monkey
47 Speak oratorically
51 Use hairclips, at the salon
55 Stand-up guy
56 Far from astute
57 Elbow bend
58 End-of-school emotion
59 First 007 film
60 Computer drop-downs
61 “Is that ___ or . . .?”
62 Egoyan’s milieus

DOWN

1 de Balboa or da Gama
2 Crazy as ___
3 School matrons of old
4 Spy’s aperture
5 Apartment bosses, briefly
6 Put on paper
7 8-Down, in Tijuana
8 Right on the map
9 Similarity
10 “This is not ___”
11 Canadian actress Campbell
12 Let off
13 US worker’s ID
18 *The Simpsons* Barney, for one
21 Seventeen-syllable poem
25 Mail sorter’s concern
26 Forsaken
27 Bourne & Kraatz and Salé & Pelletier
28 Wikipedia content, in brief
29 Jazz phrase
30 Barracks bigwigs: Abbr.
31 The day before *aujourd’hui*
32 Former Ontario premier Ernie
33 ___ noire
36 What a coupla lattes could set you back
37 Fail the acting audition, likely
38 Is following tips
44 Interlaces
45 Frozen drink brand
46 “And sometimes Y” group
47 Gift recipient
48 Agassi of the court
49 SIN card or birth cert.
50 Old PC program
51 Went like lightning
52 “___ top of the world!”
53 Women swingers club?: Abbr.
54 Like canned sardines
55 Hockey skate inits.

59 *The Mane Concern*

ACROSS

1 Jellied garnish
6 Monopoly board place
10 Movie pig
14 A clean ___
15 Anthologies or types of public transit
17 Beginning of a W.C. Fields quote
19 ___ von Bismarck
20 Light start
21 Lorry's radial
22 Part 2 of the quote
26 Meditative moans
28 Con ___ (animatedly, in music)
29 Suffix with inter-
30 Group of seven member
31 Irish martyr Robert
34 Digital readout, for short
35 Prefix meaning "ear"
36 Perrins' partner of Worcestershire sauce
37 Part 3 of the quote
41 Conductance unit
42 Let go, bluntly
43 Mason's trough
44 Actress Dianne of *Law & Order*
46 "It ___" (reply to "Who's there?")

47 Sears catalogue info.
48 Victory cry
50 French nobleman
51 Part 4 of the quote
56 *Titanic* girl
58 ___ *for Innocent* (Sue Grafton novel)
59 BC radio ranter Mair
60 End of the quote
64 Absolute
65 ___ a time (individually)
66 Campaigner's bias
67 Spanish step
68 One-pot concoctions

DOWN

1 Just ___ (pool call)
2 Extreme laziness
3 ___ Québecois
4 "I'm buying"
5 Capital of Canada
6 Noted Tory's moniker
7 Prenatal test, for short
8 ___ and outs
9 It might follow 64-Across
10 Signal on the phone
11 Hurricane Katrina evacuee site in Houston
12 Colossal creatures
13 Language suffix
16 Mean mutt

18 ASAP, in the OR
23 Style with jet-black hair and dark eyeliner
24 Sweet and high in calories
25 Pop, south of the 49th
27 "Git!"
31 Spanish war hero
32 Prove fit
33 Stuffed pasta dish
34 Business letters
38 Woeful words
39 Plantar wart location
40 Birdbrain
45 Where the pricey seats are, usually
47 Yarn unit
48 Has as a hobby
49 Bit of smoke
52 Devout
53 *Poutine* ___ (Acadian dish with grated potatoes)
54 Rule followers?
55 Fulfills, as needs
57 Canadian folk legend Rogers
60 Red Sox city, on scoreboards
61 Jack Layton's grp.
62 ___ long way (last)
63 Greek dawn goddess

60 *Following Orders*

ACROSS

1 Apply more road salt
7 UN leader Hammarskjöld
10 Wild attempt
14 Latin list-ender
15 Application question, often
16 Johnson of *Laugh-In*
17 Speaker's dais
18 With 56-Across, mom's final order
20 Goals
21 Parakeet type
23 Mom's order to a teen
29 Barbie's ex-beau
30 Gives the go-ahead
31 ___ Club (green group)
32 Logs, as data
35 They're usually high
36 Mom's order to a dad
41 Jump for Stojko
42 Appearing like
43 Place to grow grapes
46 Lush surroundings?
47 Company logos and such: Abbr.
50 Reply to 23- and 36-Across
54 Pancho's poncho
55 Switzerland's longest river
56 See 18-Across
60 Pierced, in a way
62 Seldom seen
63 Anonymous John
64 *Seinfeld* character
65 Bouillabaisse, e.g.
66 Puncture sound
67 Sines and cosines

DOWN

1 Prepare to go back home
2 Canadiens star
3 Lunatics
4 Woman in a *Paint Your Wagon* song
5 Lucy of *Charlie's Angels*
6 Any place far, far away
7 Warbucks of *Little Orphan Annie*
8 Whisky ___ (LA nightclub)
9 Gift that may be sheer?
10 Go limp
11 Angle starter
12 Off-road transport: Abbr.
13 Flower visitor
19 Garr of *Mr. Mom*
22 Spills
24 Taboo
25 Tail ends
26 Large predator often seen near Tofino, BC
27 Galena and cinnabar
28 Prepare potatoes
32 Caught sushi fish
33 Numbered hwy.
34 1984 Cyndi Lauper hit
36 Kipling mongoose Rikki-tikki-___
37 Space between leaf and stem
38 ___ Ration (dog food brand)
39 Finisher of ceramics
40 Tropical tuber
44 Promising
45 Gives in
47 Gillette razor
48 *West Side Story* Oscar winner Rita
49 Norway neighbours
51 Many lounge combos
52 Seals (up)
53 Charged
56 Husbands or wife
57 Bother, with "at"
58 "___ you for real?"
59 Untested
61 In the manner of

61 Oh, Baby!

ACROSS

1 The over-65s: Abbr.
4 Immediate surroundings
10 NHL stat
14 Chest muscle, briefly
15 Equally hip
16 Teaser's syllables
17 Are outstanding?
18 Common charley horse sites
20 Charlie Chaplin's wife
22 Peas and pellets
23 D.D.E.'s political rival
24 It might be dipped in ketchup
28 Miguel's mom
30 Banff region, for one
31 Spoken
32 Eventually
35 Makes lace
36 Newspaper newbie
39 Straight ___ arrow
41 "Ditto"
42 He has many gifts
44 For the fun of it
49 ___ Nurmi (The Flying Finn)
50 1984 martial arts film, with *The*
52 Apocryphal book: Abbr.
53 Part of an Ork greeting
55 Life sci.
56 Hunky guy or his wheels, slangily
61 NYC subway inits.
62 Mushed group?
63 Opposed
64 Young Mulroney
65 Workers' needs, in the US
66 Toyota model
67 WWW suffix

DOWN

1 *Royal Canadian Air Farce* skits
2 Design over
3 Act opener
4 Brit's raincoat
5 "Life ___ Highway" (Tom Cochrane)
6 Caesar's 650
7 Until now
8 ___ Douglas, "The Greatest Canadian"
9 Other-side-of-the-tracks area
10 Mandela's grp.
11 Vegetarian's hangout?
12 Pooh-pooh
13 Mortarboard danglers
19 A few
21 Santa ___ winds
25 Pegger's game
26 Playwright Ibsen
27 Ill-___ (doomed)
29 Funny Johnson
31 Shakespeare's *Two Gentlemen of ___*
33 Stk. market debut
34 Driving force?
36 Hoser's favourite bacon
37 Antigonish's StFX, e.g.
38 Just so
39 Features or qualities
40 Squirrels away
43 ___ out (die)
45 Neighbour of Syr.
46 With hands on hips
47 Egg-pelter, maybe
48 Singer whose name is written in lower case letters
50 Scoundrel
51 Boring tool
54 Latin "love" conjugation
57 Ruler markings: Abbr.
58 Official time signal grp.
59 Language suffix
60 Little black book no.

62 | *Phooey!* *

ACROSS

1 Salary limit
4 Mideast religion that preaches equality
9 "___ directed"
14 Poet of pugilism
15 One of three answers on a test
16 Oxygen provider
17 With 12-Down, Donald Duck's three nephews
19 Late, to Latinos
20 Brick walls, for instance
21 Beasts with brands
22 Related to mom
23 Discuss work with colleagues
25 Vied for office
26 Chow down
29 *Malcolm X* director Spike
30 Word on an invoice
31 Condense on a surface
33 Done in, like a dragon
35 Barflies
38 Poppycock
40 Looks over
41 Statue type
43 One who might grab the bull by the horns
45 Tiger's start, in two different ways
46 Israeli machine gun
48 Bay St. hub of activity
49 Vancouver Olympics annum

52 Cheers up
55 Tuck's title
57 Thick-headed
58 Mexican ranch house
61 State next to New Brunswick
62 Explosion sound
63 Doesn't miss ___ (runs smoothly)
64 Chewable Asian nut
65 Suffix with lemon, lime or orange
66 Procedures: Abbr.
67 Uses a swizzle
68 Drift off

DOWN

1 French notebook
2 Reunion attendee
3 Frisbee forerunner
4 Wicked child
5 Lincoln and Vigoda
6 Legendary Red Wing
7 "Give it ___!"
8 Dangerous for driving
9 Understandings
10 Bed boards
11 Environmentalists' celebration
12 See 17-Across
13 Gets harder to hike up
18 Chinese leader Sun ___-sen
21 Key of Québec
24 Prince ___, Saskatchewan

27 Volcano output
28 "Yer darn ___!"
31 Stupid jerk
32 Aussie hopper
34 Fifth sign of the zodiac
35 One of the Virgin Islands
36 "Sea Cruise" refrain (Frankie Ford, 1959)
37 Pacts between countries
39 Cry made with a fist-pump
42 Very beginnings
44 Gets another coffee
47 Zed, stateside
49 Ancient Cretan
50 Just managed
51 Had a look inside
53 Charge
54 Part of a bedroom set
56 Old Olds
59 Beginning drawing class
60 Trucker with a handle
62 Computer modem speed units: Abbr.

* This puzzle was taken to the summit of Mt. Everest in May, 2008. I suspect it is the only crossword ever to have reached such heights.

—DM

63 | *Season Finales*

ACROSS

1 Gomer Pyle's rank: Abbr.
4 Pushrod pushers
8 "When ___, do . . ."
14 PetroCan freebie
15 East of the Urals
16 What one monkey saw
17 Spring ___ (annual household chore)
19 Lorne of the Ponderosa
20 April 30th concern, maybe
21 Fedora feature
22 Utter stupidity
24 In, for now
25 Midlife event
28 "Listen up!"
30 *Star Trek 2* villain
33 Sri ___
34 Trigonometry function
35 Big rig
36 Tolkien tree creature
37 Screwball
40 Scalpers' items, slangily
41 Kerfuffles
43 Famous Manhattan 5th Avenue store
44 V-formation flier
46 ___ II (razor brand)
47 Absorbed, as losses
48 Changes right before your eyes, maybe
49 Hep guy
51 Puts into law
53 Fen
56 Seats fit for a king
60 Individually
61 Spring ___ (baseball's awakening)
62 Mr. Brezhnev
63 Beatles movie
64 Summer setting in Man.
65 Dogmas
66 There are two in circulation
67 Chicane shape

DOWN

1 Hostilities ender
2 TV handyman Bob
3 Mesozoic predator, for short
4 Molson product
5 Reality check phrase
6 '50s movie heartthrob Sal
7 Bend under pressure
8 Actress Swenson
9 Where to look for Polaris
10 Nike competitors
11 Spring ___ (clear the high jump)
12 Prefix with skirt or series
13 K-5
18 Take ___ (chance it)
21 Laughing scavengers
23 Spring ___ (what you aren't if you're old)
25 Soccer shoe
26 Time off, briefly
27 Spring ___ (get going)
29 Cry made with a fist-pump
31 Mennonite group
32 Puts a stop to
34 Declared as fact
38 Can. neighbour
39 Narcissists go on them
42 Like triangles with unequal sides
45 Actor, director Welles
48 Borgnine navy comedy role
50 Implied
52 Up ___ (cornered)
53 Mickey's maker
54 Blunted blade
55 Composer Rorem and actor Beatty
57 "Good work!"
58 Some are split
59 Pepper and Bilko
61 Active ingredient in pot: Abbr.

■ BARBARA OLSON

64 *Banana Split*

ACROSS

1 Hair over the forehead
6 Clearly self-satisfied
10 Humorist Bombeck
14 ___ *of Two Cities*
15 Celestial bear
16 Grace follower
17 Fit for a king
18 Rounded hammer head
19 Photos
20 Big lizard in post-op?
23 Parent's reason
24 Macdonald's bills, slangily
26 They print head lines?
27 Prov. seat holder
30 Deck section
31 ___-Sky Highway (Vancouver-Whistler connector)
33 Tennis scores after deuces
34 Supremes diva strapped for cash?
38 ___ fortune (got rich)
39 Passé
40 Cereal grains
42 Pirate's aim
43 Levin and Gershwin
47 From the earth
49 Fink on
51 Prohibit Jewish New Year
54 Baby in Baie-Comeau
55 Give the nod
56 ___ Québecois
57 Bankbook figs.
58 TV's ___ *My Ride*
59 Leave housebound, as during Quebec's winter storm of 1998
60 < to Bach: Abbr.
61 Zaire's Mobutu ___ Seko
62 "Who ___?" (apathetic comment)

DOWN

1 She's a doll
2 Drill "chill"
3 Retort to a henpecker
4 Knight with the Pips
5 Actress Ward and namesakes
6 Apartment boss, briefly
7 Talking horse of old TV
8 "___ or lose . . ."
9 India's sacred river
10 Tijuana turnover
11 Brought under control
12 Spanish line dance
13 Montreal CFLers, for short
21 Mayberry's Pyle
22 Like slave labour
25 Tire pump sound
28 Praise
29 "Canadian dollar ___" (US lure)
31 Canadien on ice
32 Palindromic Preminger
34 Fuzzy Wuzzy, for one?
35 "Aw"-inspiring?
36 Proximity
37 Winger of *Urban Cowboy*
38 Labour level: Abbr.
41 Reads your mail, say
43 Odysseus' island
44 Enthusiastic fan, maybe
45 Mommy's sis
46 Launderer's woes
48 Stamp's rival
50 Jellied garnish
52 Easter dinners
53 Biz buzz
54 English channel

65 | *Purchasing Power*

ACROSS

1 Parisian pocket money, once
6 Start of an auto insurance claim?
10 Russian port city
14 Neat freak of old TV
15 Like a mechanic's hands
16 "Fugget it!"
17 Pelican features
19 Word jumble: Abbr.
20 Ward off
21 Perfect places
22 CBC's *Maritime Noon* host Halavrezos
25 "You're darned right!"
28 Nth degree
29 Optometrist's supply
32 "Great work!" stickers
33 Chi followers
34 Ending with "smack" or "switch"
35 Bachman's boy
36 Argentina's Péron
38 Iran-Contra grp.
40 Movie set VIP
41 Barn birds
43 Eat like ___
45 Coeur d'___, Idaho
47 Gym dandy?

49 Says without thinking, with "out"
50 Hullabaloo
51 "Ready to roll?"
52 "___ Love" (The Honeydrippers)
54 Québec city near Joliette
56 Bygone sci-fi magazine
57 Cool breezes in the Canada Trust building?
62 Open or Closed, e.g.
63 Falco of *The Sopranos*
64 Some construction beams
65 Mine tram loads
66 Founded: Abbr.
67 Units of force

DOWN

1 Suffix meaning "characterized by"
2 Matter of life
3 Cabinet dept.
4 Naysayer
5 Perilous place for a rock climber
6 Yves' "eve"
7 Robbie Burns Day hirees
8 Green around the gills
9 Start to function?
10 Having been challenged, maybe

11 Holdup demands?
12 Stretch of time
13 Frat party vats
18 Better's better
21 Apocryphal book: Abbr.
22 Usual practice
23 Where Senators wear skates
24 Negligible difference
26 Failing a polygraph
27 Opposite of 1-Down
30 ___-Claire, QB
31 Least likely to kiss and make up
33 Of the Vatican
37 Temptress
39 Phone prankster's foil
42 Certain winners
44 Huffy
46 Brahms offering
48 Comics punch line?
49 Shakespeare, for one
52 Middle-of-the-road
53 Dubai dignitary
55 Gave the nod
57 Seinfeld's ___ *Movie*
58 Classified info
59 One who follows the stars
60 *Uno + due*
61 Snake's sound

66 Order, Order!

ACROSS

1 Suspension bridge support
6 Thai money
10 No. on a bank statement
14 Kind of flu
15 "I could ___ horse!"
16 Scott of sitcoms
17 If you incite one, 58-Across may result
19 ___ account (never)
20 Swellhead's trait
21 You'll see CBC on it
22 Cry of wonderment
25 Like new, in used car ads
26 Sounds at the Canadian Grand Prix
27 Over the line
29 Charles Lamb's pen name
31 Wray of *King Kong* (1933)
32 Regarding, to attorneys
33 Have an early peek
35 Card game with melds
38 Figure on a tax return
41 Blue movies
43 Spanish miss: Abbr.
44 Winter hrs. in Cape Breton
46 Laze about
47 Yuppie's wheels, often
49 Accident
51 Breezed through, as an exam
53 Place to pamper oneself
54 Word before city or circle
55 Juan de Fuca is one
57 Fizzles (out)
58 Total lack of order
62 Radiator sound
63 Veto from Putin
64 ___-Neuve (province bordering Québec)
65 Head of the Parti Québécois?
66 Parched
67 The RAF, in a famous speech by Churchill

DOWN

1 Ferry load
2 "___ live and breathe!"
3 A short life's story
4 Past the deadline
5 The Soviet Union, to Churchill
6 Get started
7 House pet with an exercise wheel
8 Film director Egoyan
9 Check for drinks
10 From the beginning: Lat.
11 If you open them, 58-Across may result
12 Cannes focus
13 Little piggy's place: Var.
18 Film genre
21 It's in your genes
22 Narc or psych ending
23 Mrs. Chaplin
24 If you disturb it, 58-Across may result
26 "___ *le roi!*"
28 Powerful political tool
30 Olin of *Havana*
33 Sandbox toy
34 Apart from this
36 Kind of panel
37 Feature of some 'Vettes
39 Part of a flight
40 Cupcake maker ___ Lee
42 Din
44 In the thick of
45 Gary of *Forrest Gump*
47 Put up with
48 Official proclamations
50 *Steppenwolf* writer
52 Minotaur's home
55 Eye annoyance
56 Lt. Kojak, to friends
58 Young '___ (kids)
59 Bow-wow's kin
60 Smelter input
61 Buttonhole, in a way

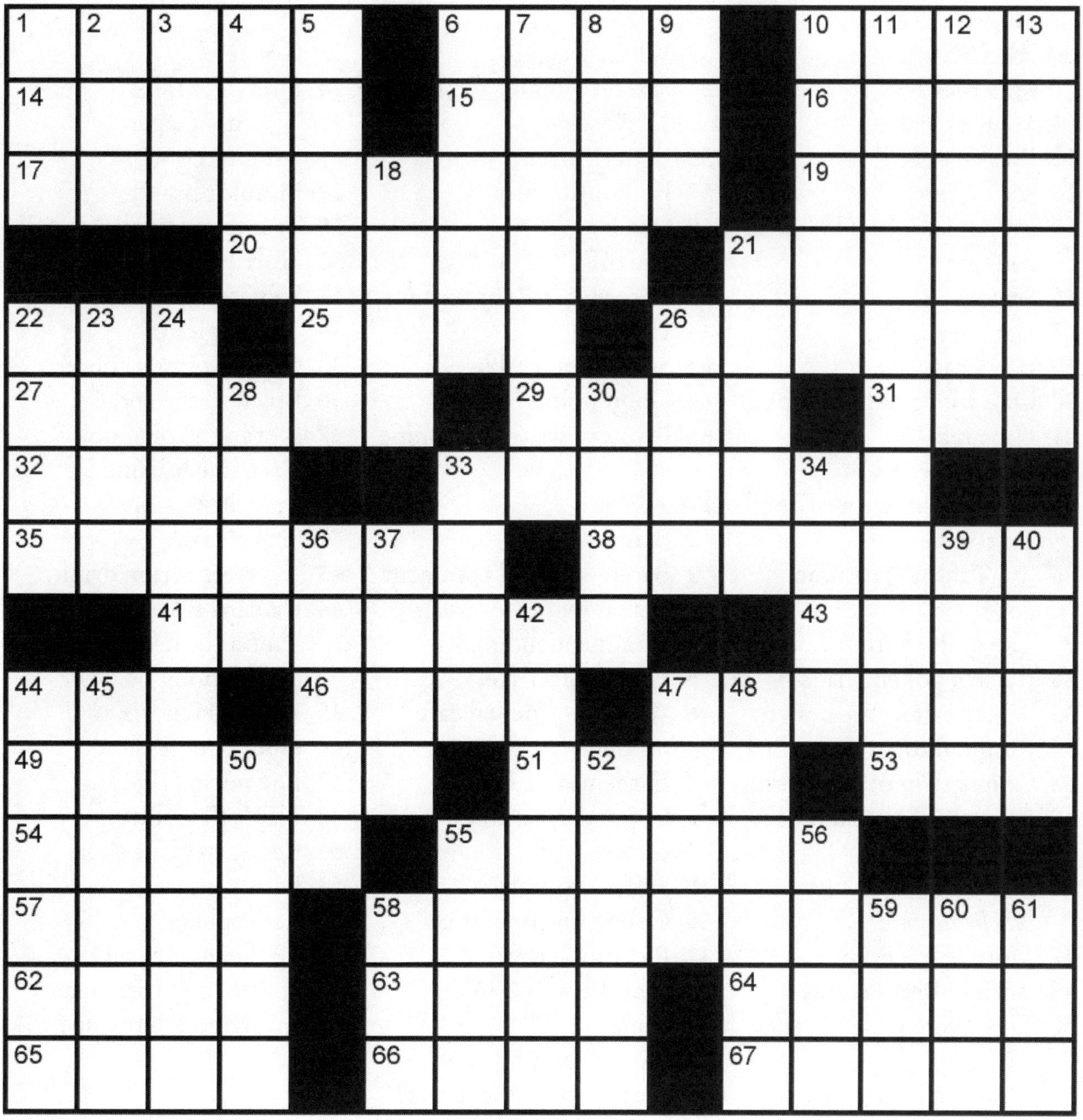

67 The Moral of the Story

ACROSS

1 Meter leader
4 Medical vial
10 Pressing need
14 Sci-fi fliers
15 Brand name in Chinese cooking
16 Sew up
17 Start of a quip
19 Each, casually
20 One with a tail, perhaps
21 Hip area
23 Biographer Leon
24 Berton who wrote *The Last Spike*
26 ___ Tafaria (Jamaican god)
29 The quip continues …
32 It's in a poker's hand
33 Where sailors are drawn
34 Respond to, as an instinct
38 Comic strip office worker
40 Former CBC Radio host Jackson
41 Mozart's ___ *Kleine Nachtmusik*
42 More of the quip
49 Born in Beaupré, say
50 They were wide in the '70s
51 Result of using one's *tête*
52 Wheat weight
54 "Sweet Child ___" (Guns N' Roses)
55 Potter's oven
57 End of the quip
60 "Suck ___!"
61 Tee off
62 *Rosemary's Baby* writer Levin
63 Small time?: Abbr.
64 Good points
65 Mystery writer Josephine

DOWN

1 Blast rock, maybe
2 Barely satisfied comment
3 Out at night?
4 Comment ending?
5 First quarter mo.
6 Water ___ (dental care product)
7 In the near distance
8 County in central Ontario
9 Suffer through
10 Colourful computer
11 Put another way
12 John Lennon's middle name
13 House party?
18 "Have you decided yet?"
22 Got cozy
24 Firebug, briefly
25 "___ it!" (eager volunteer's words)
27 Monitor brand
28 Trump card game
30 Horrifies
31 Something to do
34 ___ Eagleson
35 Cryptologist's concern
36 Loyal to the end
37 Not in the ph. book
38 Certain bar name
39 Traveller's stops
41 Snake's lack
43 ___ mama (rum drink)
44 Richard Bradshaw Amphitheatre productions
45 Rock's Hendrix
46 Guilty confession
47 Poe poem (1831)
48 Plan's flexibility
53 Racist, say, for short
54 Fesses (up)
55 Kith cousin
56 "___ been a slice!"
58 Start of a musical scale
59 In a lather, with "up"

68 B-o-o-ring

ACROSS

1 Jet-black, in verse
5 Rocking Turner
9 Twisting turns
14 Superboy's sweetheart Lang
15 Gem for a Libra, maybe
16 Blues singer Bonnie
17 Like garage-sale items
18 "Just say ___ drugs." (Nancy Reagan)
19 Fur coat sporter
20 * Slim pickings, e.g.
23 Give a hoot
24 Contrive, as a plot
25 1930s-50s Arab ruler
28 Indian restaurant appetizer
32 Ending with schnozz
33 Like May to August, compared with other months
36 "I'll get right ___"
37 Blacktop goo
38 They're b-o-o-ring (like the first words of the starred clue answers)
41 "Yo te ___"
42 Wile E. Coyote's supplier
44 "Ouch!"
45 Turntable letters
46 '70s space station
49 Mercury's had wings
51 Move in on
54 Not all
55 * 1980 Best Picture with Mary Tyler Moore
60 Nunavut resident
61 Polar-bear prey
62 Lecturer's platform
63 Helsinki coin
64 Actress Garr
65 Kodak competitor
66 Surfboard fins
67 Green Gables lass
68 Middle middle

DOWN

1 Twelfth Hebrew month
2 * Old CBC radio show hosted by humorist Arthur
3 Rambo, as a combatant
4 Lowest points
5 Muscle quality
6 Apple with tunes
7 "You betcha!"
8 Don Ho's hi
9 Nickname of Beethoven's Third Symphony
10 Louis Armstrong's nickname
11 Web spot
12 Dog days in Drummondville
13 Orchestral grp.
21 Emotional
22 Fourth periods in hockey, briefly
25 Mere specks
26 Ending with form
27 Moist in the morning
29 Like Godzilla stomping Tokyo
30 * Paris Hilton show, with "The"
31 They split when they're smashed
34 Cone or Cat preceder
35 Has in stitches
39 Small inlet
40 One of five, or maybe six
43 Giving the slip to
47 The way things stand
48 Patty's place
50 Thingy
52 Dreadlocks wearer
53 Primp
55 Short jog, for short
56 Ancient letter
57 Old gob's tale
58 Ballet bend
59 Those, to José
60 VCR speed measure: Abbr.

69 The Ins Are Out

ACROSS

1 "Hey, over here!"
5 Bury in a grave
11 Commons people: Abbr.
14 Symptom of 38-Across
15 Fasten with a click
16 Acorn producer
17 Vet bills and kibble costs for the mutt?
19 Classical grp. at the Orpheum
20 Flexible
21 Result of drying out, maybe
22 Greek pizza topping
23 Tools of old math
24 "Love ___ Many-Splendored ..."
25 Show great anticipation
26 College fees for females?
29 Old Eur. domain
30 Beer parlour
31 Freeway access
34 All that one can carry
38 Rash cause
42 Chem. suffix
43 Money to purchase clerical robes?
46 Renders speechless
48 Off-road rig
49 "Spine" of Chile
50 http:// addresses
51 Clairvoyant's claim
52 Lute look-alike
53 Face, slangily
54 Not qualified for the convent?
57 Celestial altar
58 Connects
59 Attired
60 Dominic Da Vinci, e.g.: Abbr.
61 Builds an in-law suite, say
62 Shift and enter, e.g.

DOWN

1 Photo
2 Mule-like
3 Horror movie viewer's annoyance, maybe
4 Subsequently, old-style
5 Kids' guessing game
6 180 degrees from SSW
7 Cops 'n' robbers cry
8 Like many a bedroom or apartment
9 Homer's hangouts
10 Canadian duo?
11 Get over, as a heartbreak
12 Milano meal
13 Chewing tobacco brand
18 Marked on a bingo card, once
22 *Escape from Freedom* author Erich
23 *Horton Hears* ___
24 "Give ___ rest!"
25 Designer Christian
27 Mar. honouree
28 Lift one's spirits?
32 Grace words
33 Angler's haul
35 Not a good hider
36 Carpet padding
37 Suffix meaning "without"
39 Blotto
40 Pull into the slow lane, say
41 SASE part: Abbr.
43 Lewd
44 ___ accompli
45 Pull the pin?
46 Cashew family shrub
47 Nova Scotia town
51 Woman in Tennyson's *Idylls of the King*
52 ___ Fein
54 Actress Hagen
55 Book jacket blurb
56 Broadbent and Stelmach

■ DAVE MACLEOD

70 Don't Be a Brat

ACROSS

1 Plant seeds
4 UN figure: Abbr.
7 Long-nosed jet, briefly
10 Gaping mouth
13 Leader of tomorrow
14 Devoted fan
16 Pub potable
17 It makes a man mean?
18 Brat's answer to "Go cut the lawn"
20 Alpine call
22 Army creatures?
23 Skin product prefix
25 ___ de plume
26 Spaceship's escape vehicles
29 Starting from
31 Believer's suffix
34 Media baron Murdoch
36 Little pay
40 Brat's answer to "Take out the trash"
42 11th-13th century invader
43 Portly
44 Really poor grades
45 Head light?
47 Hot times in Québec
48 Feathery scarf
51 Big city suburbs, often
53 Mexican musicians
57 Schoolboy collars
61 Brat's answer to "Make your bed"
63 Slangy denial
64 Superman archenemy Luthor
65 Baseball round-tripper
66 Cassowary cousin
67 One or more
68 Brillo alternative
69 Peter, Paul and Mary: Abbr.
70 Collector's goal

DOWN

1 Command to Fido
2 Vintner's prefix
3 Garden nuisance
4 Spry
5 Actor in chains
6 Heart locations
7 Popular Dalmatian name
8 Keep under wraps
9 Allegro or adagio
10 Capts.' superiors
11 Skin soother
12 Fly traps
15 Like brats, usually
19 "Tasty!"
21 '50s Ford flops
24 Deserved
26 Vincent of horror flicks
27 Pretty weird
28 Poor grade
30 Tree that's named Douglas, e.g.
31 Data to enter
32 Play part
33 Sees to
35 Genetic info carrier
37 Have, as a hissy fit
38 Eastern "way"
39 Most likely
41 Car, truck or bus: Abbr.
46 Also-rans
48 Osama ___ Laden
49 You curse and swear in using them
50 It may initiate a blessing
52 Colourful aquarium fish
53 Ms. Mulroney
54 Capital of Yemen
55 Classic theatre name
56 They don't get Oscars
58 Individuals
59 Moniker
60 Word with up or down
62 King played by Steve Martin

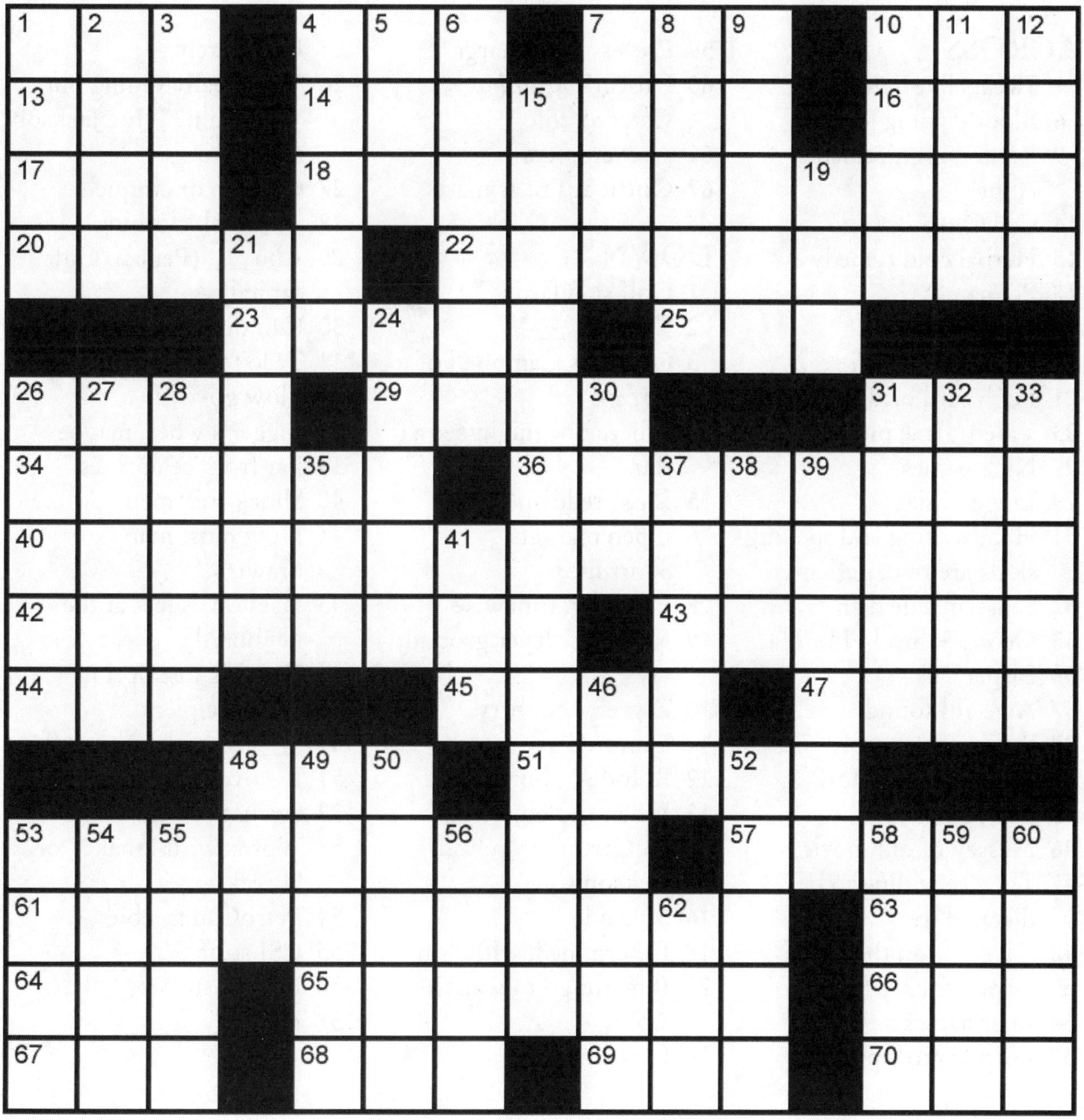

■ BARBARA OLSON

71 | *Name-calling*

ACROSS

1 Sweats like a dog
6 Blood-typing letters
9 Refund requirements: Abbr.
14 Old Olds
15 Herbal cold remedy
17 Pet names
19 Helmsman
20 Opposite of *adios*
21 High card bridge combo
23 Video-game pioneer
27 Nick names
29 Lingerie size
31 Handwriting and spelling skills are two, perhaps
32 Seussian side dish
33 George's bro in Florida
36 Lisper's Ss
37 Awe-ful sound?
38 Willing to comply
41 Point of a pitchfork
42 Pen names
46 Massey of old movies
47 They're willing to be dictated to
48 Give ___ on the back
50 Caped trick-or-treater
54 First names?
58 For the most part
59 Professeur's charge
60 Dustin's *Midnight Cowboy* role
61 Ave. crossers
62 Outfit again, as masts

DOWN

1 Golf standards
2 "Thanks ___!"
3 Canada's Campbell of *Scream*
4 Where one might see a star
5 Light reddish-brown
6 Open markets
7 Short life?
8 Precisely, timewise
9 Moves to dryer ground, say
10 Zagreb's country
11 Tammy Faye's grp.
12 Rolodex abbr.
13 When tripled, a Paul McCartney/Michael Jackson song
16 Mil. aide
18 Determined, with "on"
22 It might go to waist?: Abbr.
24 Deft
25 Be a snitch
26 "___ Really Going out With Him?" (Joe Jackson song)
27 Quattro or cinque
28 ___ Kosh clothing
29 Abu ___ (Persian Gulf capital)
30 Camouflage colour
33 Taco topper
34 Flow go-with
35 Jogger's woes, maybe
39 Far from celebrities
40 Shock treatment: Abbr.
41 How most maps are drawn
43 Uses one's feet at the keyboard
44 Crucifix inscription
45 IOU recipient
49 "___ Maria"
51 It's over for Otto
52 Strauss of denim
53 Words with "shake" or "break"
54 PetroCan freebie
55 CSI stuff
56 Real estate rep.
57 Hep guy

146

■ DAVE MACLEOD

72 Say "Cheese"

ACROSS

1 Cheese that has "eyes"
8 Quell concerns
14 Jennifer of *Friends*
15 Tied up at the dock
16 Break up, as a crowd
18 It's on the tip of your tongue
19 Suit to ___
20 Virtual city computer games
22 *The Divine* ___ (Bette Midler album)
23 A sock in the jaw, slangily
26 Persona non ___
29 U-turn from WSW
30 Apple on a desk, maybe
34 Sock-in-the-gut grunt
35 Light-headed?
38 Folded fast food
39 Hagen of stage and screen
40 Carlos at Woodstock
42 Bald Brynner
43 Medics
45 Warm up, as leftovers
46 Bay St. wheeler-dealer
47 Side squared, for squares
48 When doubled, a dance
49 "Suppose..."
51 Recover furniture
55 Shore up

58 1998 Australian Open tennis winner Korda
59 "Now ___ me down ..."
63 Kitchen plan
65 Bad bunch in *Mad Max* (1979)
67 "Um ... sure"
68 "Didn't you hear me the first time?"
69 Liveliness
70 Cheese that can bite

DOWN

1 "If I ___ Hammer"
2 Have ___ to pick
3 Carpentry clamp
4 Viewpoint
5 Bus driver's assignment: Abbr.
6 Statues with no arms, sometimes: Var.
7 Against moral teachings
8 Morning hrs.
9 Me too
10 Formally request
11 *QB VII* author
12 Guns, as a motor
13 Cheese that's made backwards?
17 Cheese with holes
21 Malt-shop purchase

24 Montréal Canadiens, to fans
25 "... ___ ghost!"
26 Cheese that's a big wheel
27 Chopper blade
28 "I've Just Seen ___" (Beatles)
31 Ancient Mexicans
32 Integra maker
33 Cheese that won't bite
36 Tamarack
37 Like an easy grounder or a short trip
41 Even, after "in"
44 More impudent
50 Giving the cold shoulder
52 Britney Spears sold it
53 Impassive
54 It's down in the dumps
55 Cheese to party with
56 Brief bylaws
57 "Care for ___ of tea?"
60 Actor Alan or Cheryl
61 The "*I*" of *The King and I*
62 Lugosi role in *Son of Frankenstein*
64 Toronto "fall back" hrs.
66 2000 Peace Nobelist Kim ___ Jung

73 *It's a Mad Scramble*

ACROSS

1 Barbecued finger food
9 Shabby shacks
15 Bleacher's solution
16 Single file
17 One who "struts and frets" upon a stage, perhaps
18 Add one's two cents, in a sense
19 Qty. of eggs
20 Size of eggs: Abbr.
22 Major finish
23 Home for the holidays
26 Bathroom bar brand
28 Toaster's opening
30 Your guess ___ good ...
31 Legend ending
32 Bear, in Bolivia
34 Female vampire
38 Helps Farmer Jones at harvest time?
43 Prohibitive words
44 Ste.-___ (Québec city)
45 Hot Point rivals
46 Like Victoria's Secret items
49 Fine diner
52 Initiate, as a project
56 Matane misses, for short
57 Burn black
58 Capable, slangily

59 Swingers' club? Abbr.
60 Helicopter parts
62 Keep separately, as pin money
67 Bless by applying oil
68 Ideal model
69 It's "manic" in a Bangles song
70 Post slopes chill-out

DOWN

1 Round solid: Abbr.
2 Word with snap or snow
3 Provide with heat?
4 Band aid
5 They're out of the cooler
6 Swanky hotel, with "the"
7 Bachelor's last words
8 Comedian Milton
9 Seeker's quarry, in a kid's game
10 Lennon's love
11 Actress Redgrave, and others
12 Muse with a lyre
13 A ___ (tons o')
14 Curler's call
21 Happy, to Henri
23 Leafy beet
24 *Correo* ___ (Spanish airmail)

25 Rocker Adams from Kingston, ON
26 A Spice Girl
27 Red-tag event
29 Auto wrecker's service
33 Brutish clod
35 Ski bump
36 "If ___ you, ..." (advisor's words)
37 Some burden bearers
39 Former instant camera brand
40 Sheriff's pin-on
41 Pigeon-___
42 Rt.-angled triangle abbr.
47 Buxom
48 "Yer darn tootin'"
50 "Count me in!"
51 Grips firmly
52 "Beat it!"
53 Prefix with -graph
54 Major Toronto shopping centre
55 Baffled
59 Prefix meaning "winged"
61 Genetic strand
63 Best before abbr.
64 The guys, to Guy
65 US state starting with S. or N.
66 "___ tu" (Verdi aria)

74 *In Living Colour*

ACROSS

1 Mourns loudly
6 Lunkheads
11 Be busily active
14 Northern residence
15 Have ___ to play
16 Whichever
17 Having a sad time
19 Family girl
20 Loyal or royal follower
21 Halifax harbour sight
22 *Arsenic and ___*
24 *High* ___ (early pot magazine)
26 Roll with a hole
27 Wears a scowl
32 Bushy coif
33 Owner's paper
34 Vidal of shampoos
38 Bun toppers
43 Lead-up to a coup
45 Huff and puff
46 Wish you had what they have
53 Canadian smell
54 Broadcast sign
55 Falls between two countries?
58 Letters before an afterthought
59 Discredited news broadcaster
62 Part of NATO: Abbr.
63 Makes happy as a clam
66 "You don't mean me?!"
67 ___ vincit amor
68 Start of a counting-out rhyme
69 Outrage
70 Overrun with cattails
71 Barbecue skewers

DOWN

1 Kind of connection for travelling computer users
2 A very long time
3 ABBA's "___ the Music Speak"
4 Cyber-guffaw
5 "You're right after all"
6 Partner of a cloak
7 Poet's planet
8 Game requiring horse sense
9 Twelfth Hebrew month
10 Places of growth and development
11 Takes one's turn
12 Worldwide relief org.
13 "All By ___": Céline Dion hit
18 Insensitive
23 Young fella
24 They stop fights, briefly
25 Cover ground, in a way
27 Spanish article
28 One ___ kind
29 IV sites
30 *Scream* director Craven
31 Alumna bio word
35 Wheeler-dealer
36 Bullring bravo
37 Québec referendum word
39 Takeoff artist
40 Beatnik's exasperated exclamation
41 Part of SASE: Abbr.
42 Porker's pen
44 The only even prime number
46 Good friend, to Gaston
47 Newspaper doyen
48 "The puck stops here" player
49 Slangy toupee
50 Like a live ball
51 Hard-to-refute evidence
52 Greets the villain
56 Frosty coating
57 Teen woe
59 Over in France
60 "I'll get right ___"
61 Classic Jaguar sports cars
64 ___ *Galahad* (Elvis film)
65 Get-up-and-go

75 *Famous Last Words*

ACROSS

1 Kim's Sussex Drive successor
5 Orajel target
9 Forgetful letter writer's letters
13 Prince Harry's aunt
14 Make ___ stop
15 Isle in the Firth of Clyde
16 Old-school schooling
17 Script bit
18 First word of "Irish Lullaby"
19 Narnia boy's *Prince Caspian* title, with "King"
22 "Mountain Music" band
24 "Isn't ___ bit like you ... ?" (Beatles lyric)
25 Jiffy
26 Rolex invention of 1929
29 Suffix with morph- and phon-
30 Initials on a bow
31 Halifax Highland Games headgear
32 It may be felt at Niagara Falls
35 "*Sprechen* ___ *Deutsch*?"
37 Belonging to youse
41 Registrant's charge
43 They're split in bananas
45 "I've told you ___ thousand times"
46 "I'm in no mood for your sass!"
52 Rolodex info
53 Middle Earth menace
54 Ties a double bow
55 Speaker of the phrase revealed by the last words of 19-, 26- and 46-Across
58 Takes too much, briefly
59 Juan's eager assent
60 Dosage amts.
63 Short squabble
64 Hunter's moon mos.
65 "___ mouse!"
66 Canadian gas brand
67 Light meal
68 Like a new non-smoker, maybe

DOWN

1 Kid's makeshift aquarium
2 Antacid brand
3 Big-nosed Australian?
4 If ___ (only when required)
5 Word coined by Lewis Carroll meaning to tread clumsily
6 Vigorously protesting
7 Give a hoot
8 Prefix meaning "chest"
9 Sci. fair exhibit, for example
10 French novelist Marcel
11 About 3.26 light-years
12 Steal, as a purse
15 Eroded
20 Scratch the surface, maybe
21 Heavy weight
22 Blows away, in a way
23 It can brighten a room
27 Wicker willow
28 Latin lover's word
33 Skipper's rear end
34 Hard kind of question for a fence-sitter
36 Puts one's faith in
38 Expelled from a dwelling
39 Easy win
40 Scot's nots
42 Raison d'___
44 Born Bjorn?
46 Oust from office
47 Rust and lime, for two
48 Atomic tryouts, briefly
49 Responds to, as an instinct
50 ___ d'Anticosti, Gulf of St. Lawrence
51 Just so
56 ___-Rooter
57 Rich, to Ricardo
61 Purolator delivery: Abbr.
62 Get off one's chest

■ BARBARA OLSON & DAVE MACLEOD

1 ■ Cool Cuisine

2 ■ Android's Puzzle

3 ■ Not Again!

4 ■ Starry, Starry Night

5 ■ Ety-mology

O	M	A	N		R	O	T	S		U	P	A	N	D
R	A	V	I		E	L	S	E		N	H	L	E	R
E	X	E	C		N	A	P	E		H	O	P	E	S
L	I	C	K	E	T	Y	S	P	L	I	T			
			E	V	A			A	T	O	N	E	S	
		C	L	I	C	K	E	T	Y	C	L	A	C	K
D	E	E		L	O	A	M	Y		H	A	N	O	I
H	A	L	T		P	R	E	P	S		B	O	L	L
A	R	L	E	S		A	R	E	A	L		O	I	L
B	L	A	N	K	E	T	Y	B	L	A	N	K		
I	S	R	A	E	L			U	Z	I				
		C	L	I	P	P	E	T	Y	C	L	O	P	
B	A	G	I	T		Y	O	R	E		E	U	R	O
U	N	I	T	E		R	E	A	R		S	K	E	E
S	A	T	Y	R		E	M	T	S		T	E	S	T

6 ■ For Crying Out Loud

7 ■ And Sometimes Y

8 ■ Starting with the ABCs

■ BARBARA OLSON & DAVE MACLEOD

9 ■ *Cheep Talk*

```
A S A ▪ A H I L L ▪ P S A L M
M A D E W A V E S ▪ I O T A S
B L O C K H E A D ▪ A F O O T
E S P O ▪ A G R ▪ A N T ▪ ▪ ▪
R A T ▪ P H O N Y D O C T O R
▪ ▪ C O A T ▪ O H S ▪ I R E
M A C R O ▪ G R O ▪ D E A D
O B S E R V E S E C R E T L Y
S A P S ▪ A M T ▪ A P O S E
H B O ▪ R N A ▪ C C C P ▪ ▪
E A T H U N G R I L Y ▪ T H O
▪ ▪ O N A ▪ A C E ▪ C R O P
A C H O O ▪ G R E A T T I M E
S N A F U ▪ P E R T U R B E D
P S S S T ▪ A R O S E ▪ E R S
```

10 ■ *Tasty Turnovers*

```
A C A N ▪ A H E A D ▪ S A L A
D O N O ▪ W O L F E ▪ E B A Y
D R Y M E A S U R E ▪ M U G S
I N D O O R P L U M B I N G ▪
N E A R S ▪ ▪ I S A ▪ D A R
G A Y E ▪ E R S T ▪ D E A R S
▪ ▪ O R C A ▪ A G E N D A
▪ I M P E A C H M E N T ▪
P A D R E S ▪ R U E R ▪ ▪
B R A I N ▪ C O R N ▪ F A H D
S U R ▪ I M E ▪ E L D E R
▪ G E T T I N G U P E A R L Y
G U Y S ▪ S T A L A G M I T E
S L O P ▪ T R I A L ▪ E V E R
T A U S ▪ S E A N S ▪ S E R S
```

11 ■ *Choo Choo!*

```
R A W D E A L ▪ T L C ▪ S E S
F R A I L T Y ▪ O O O ▪ E D T
S K Y D I V E ▪ D O G S A G E
▪ ▪ S S S ▪ G D P ▪ T W E E
A B A T H ▪ H O L Y G R A I L
J O N ▪ A R U L E ▪ P A Y N E
A N N A ▪ O E D ▪ T A U ▪ ▪
R A I L W A Y C R O S S I N G
▪ ▪ L O N ▪ A O K ▪ S O U R
S A W T O ▪ P R M E N ▪ U K R
T R A I L R I D E ▪ O A S E S
E T Y M ▪ E G S ▪ T R U ▪ ▪
P I L E S U P ▪ B A W D I E R
P E A ▪ O S E ▪ B R A I L L E
E R Y ▪ B E N ▪ L A Y S L O W
```

12 ■ *Crossword Construction 101*

```
S C A R F ▪ N O T V ▪ K O O L
H O L E R ▪ O B O E ▪ N A R Y
A M I C I ▪ M I S T ▪ E K G S
D E V I S E A T H E M E ▪ ▪
S T E P K I D S ▪ R E H E A T
▪ ▪ E E N ▪ E A T I N T O
W T S ▪ D E S I G N A G R I D
A R U G ▪ O D E ▪ H O M O
F I L L I N W O R D S ▪ N E S
T A K E N O N ▪ A L A ▪ ▪
S L Y E S T ▪ R U T A B A G A
▪ C O M P O S E C L U E S ▪
O V A L ▪ A N D I ▪ K A T E Y
O A H U ▪ N E I N ▪ E R O S E
F L A B ▪ Y U N G ▪ R E S E T
```

13 ■ Films for the Family

G	R	P	S	■	S	I	B	S	■	L	A	D	E	N
R	E	E	K	■	A	P	O	P	■	O	V	I	N	E
A	P	R	I	L	F	O	O	L	■	R	A	T	S	O
M	O	M	M	I	E	D	E	A	R	E	S	T	■	■
P	R	I	S	M	■	■	R	T	E	■	T	Y	P	E
A	T	T	■	E	F	G	■	S	O	S	■	B	U	Y
■	■	C	A	R	A	T	■	■	I	N	A	N	E	■
■	D	A	D	D	Y	L	O	N	G	L	E	G	S	■
M	O	R	S	E	■	■	D	A	N	K	E	■	■	■
G	O	B	■	S	H	A	■	N	U	I	■	C	T	R
B	R	O	W	■	O	R	C	■	■	E	I	E	I	O
■	■	R	O	S	E	M	A	R	Y	S	B	A	B	Y
F	I	E	R	O	■	A	N	A	S	T	A	S	I	A
A	L	A	S	T	■	D	I	N	E	■	R	E	A	L
B	E	L	T	S	■	A	S	T	R	■	S	S	S	S

14 ■ Humour That's Over Your Head

Ⓖ	O	E	S	■	L	A	T	C	H	■	E	L	S	E
P	U	L	P	■	I	N	Y	O	U	R	F	A	C	E
A	T	E	R	M	F	O	R	W	R	Ⓘ	T	T	E	N
■	C	A	M	E	T	O	■	R	O	S	E	N	■	■
G	E	T	W	I	S	E	■	E	A	T	■	Ⓡ	E	A
T	H	E	L	I	P	■	U	N	H	E	R	O	I	C
S	S	E	■	Ⓐ	E	R	O	■	R	U	N	I	C	■
■	■	V	A	N	D	A	L	I	S	M	■	■	■	■
Ⓕ	U	S	E	D	■	A	L	A	N	■	■	Ⓕ	A	D
O	P	E	N	A	R	M	S	■	S	P	R	I	N	T
U	S	A	■	P	E	S	■	S	E	L	E	C	T	S
■	T	R	O	T	S	■	A	T	C	O	S	T	■	■
P	A	I	N	Ⓣ	E	D	V	E	R	Y	H	I	G	H
N	I	N	E	O	N	E	O	N	E	■	Ⓘ	O	T	A
E	R	G	S	■	D	O	N	O	T	■	P	N	O	M

15 ■ O Canada

E	S	T	A	T	E	■	■	B	I	R	T	H	O	F
N	A	I	L	I	N	■	N	O	N	E	V	E	N	T
R	I	B	B	E	D	■	E	X	C	E	S	S	E	S
I	L	I	E	■	■	B	R	O	A	D	■	■	■	■
C	H	A	R	T	E	R	O	F	R	I	G	H	T	S
H	O	S	T	I	L	E	■	■	S	T	I	E	R	S
■	■	■	F	E	E	L	A	■	■	G	R	O	S	■
■	C	O	N	F	E	D	E	R	A	T	I	O	N	■
E	A	V	E	■	■	S	I	N	G	A	■	■	■	■
T	R	E	B	E	K	■	E	N	R	A	G	E	S	■
C	O	N	S	T	I	T	U	T	I	O	N	A	C	T
■	■	A	M	O	S	T	■	■	A	R	A	R	■	■
S	H	A	L	L	O	T	S	■	S	C	L	E	R	A
R	E	T	A	I	N	E	R	■	S	P	O	T	T	Y
A	N	A	T	I	O	N	■	■	H	U	G	H	E	S

16 ■ Words from the Bard?

D	E	E	M	■	S	A	L	A	M	I	■	A	U	S
O	T	R	O	■	A	C	I	D	I	C	■	I	N	E
O	T	I	C	■	R	E	T	A	K	E	■	D	R	E
M	U	C	H	A	D	O	■	■	A	B	A	S	E	S
■	■	■	A	S	I	F	■	A	D	E	P	T	A	T
C	U	E	S	I	N	■	■	T	O	R	N	A	D	O
P	I	X	■	P	I	E	C	E	■	G	E	T	■	■
R	E	T	D	■	A	B	O	U	T	■	A	I	M	S
■	■	R	I	N	■	O	N	P	O	P	■	O	A	T
B	R	A	V	A	D	O	■	■	R	U	I	N	E	D
R	A	N	A	M	O	K	■	M	T	N	S	■	■	■
O	P	E	N	E	R	■	■	N	O	T	H	I	N	G
I	T	O	■	T	A	I	P	E	I	■	T	S	A	R
L	O	U	■	A	D	D	A	M	S	■	A	S	E	A
S	R	S	■	G	O	A	T	E	E	■	R	O	S	Y

17 ■ *What a Racket!*

18 ■ *Do the Shuffle*

19 ■ *Things in Common*

20 ■ *Water, Water, Everywhere*

A	S	I		A	L	T	H	O		S	T	E	P	S
S	L	A		C	I	A	O	S		L	E	N	I	N
H	I	G	H	(H)	(H)	O	R	S	E		O	N	C	L	E
A	D	R	I	E	N	N	E			A	T	T	L	E	E
M	E	E	T				R	U	S	H	(H)	(H)	O	U	R
E	S	E		A	L	S		P	S	S		S	P	A
			S	P	E	C	T	R	A		F	E	S	T
	R	O	U	G	(H)	(H)	O	U	S	E	S			
E	T	A	T		R	O	Y	A	L	T	Y			
D	U	G		C	O	O		R	T	S		B	R	S
W	I	T	(H)	(H)	O	L	D				B	R	A	E
A	T	R	I	U	M		R	I	G	A	T	O	N	I
R	I	A	N	T		F	I	S	(H)	(H)	O	O	K	S
D	O	D	G	E		D	E	N	I	M		D	I	M
I	N	E	E	D		A	D	O	Z	E		S	N	O

21 ■ Over the Top

M	A	I	M		E	G	A	D		S	P	O	T	S
E	L	M	O		B	E	L	A		H	E	A	R	A
N	A	N	U		B	L	O	W	S	O	U	T	O	F
D	I	O	N	N	E		E	N	T	R		E	V	E
		T	A	D	A			A	T	O	N	E	S	
A	O	K	A	Y		S	H	A	R	I	F			
O	M	N	I		A	R	I	S	E		A	D	A	M
N	E	O	N		M	A	K	E	A		M	U	S	E
E	N	T	O		A	R	E	N	T		O	D	I	E
		U	T	T	E	R	S		C	L	E	F	T	
T	E	E	T	H	E		E	N	C	E				
Y	A	N		R	U	S	S		A	S	H	A	M	E
P	R	O	P	O	R	T	I	O	N		I	L	I	A
E	L	L	E	N		E	T	N	A		L	I	E	S
B	Y	A	G	E		M	E	S	S		L	I	N	E

22 ■ It's Music to My Ears

M	V	P		S	I	T	P	A	T		A	J	O	B
A	I	R		H	O	A	R	S	E		P	U	L	L
S	T	O	L	E	N	B	A	S	S		U	N	D	O
H	O	V	E		M	O	T	E		O	F	T		
	S	T	A	T	U	S	C	Y	M	B	A	L	S	
	S	W	A	N			I	O	W	A				
P	R	E		O	R	I	O	L	E		N	A	M	E
P	E	D	A	L	S	O	N	E	S	W	A	R	E	S
P	A	I	R		I	N	T	O	T	O		D	S	T
	M	B	A	S			N	A	N	A				
B	E	L	L	O	F	T	H	E	B	A	L	L		
O	D	E		D	I	R	E			A	E	R	O	
Z	O	O	T		B	O	W	B	R	I	D	G	E	S
O	U	I	S		E	V	E	N	E	D		U	N	I
S	T	L	O		R	E	D	A	T	E		P	T	S

23 ■ Porcine Parade

D	O	A		K	I	T	E	R		P	S	A	L	M
I	N	S	I	N	C	E	R	E		A	N	D	E	S
S	W	I	N	E	H	E	R	D		N	O	D	A	T
M	A	T	T	E			T	O	D	O	S			
A	R	I	L		P	I	G	I	N	A	P	O	K	E
Y	D	S		G	L	A	R	E	S		N	E	T	
		D	R	O	M	E		M	A	T	E	S		
	C	A	N	A	D	I	A	N	B	A	C	O	N	
I	L	I	A	D		T	O	O	T	H				
M	E	R		D	O	E	S	I	T		S	H	A	
P	O	R	K	B	A	R	R	E	L		E	L	E	V
	A	L	A	M	P			S	T	A	L	E		
A	L	I	E	N		H	O	G	H	E	A	V	E	N
M	E	D	I	C		A	N	O	I	N	T	I	N	G
Y	E	S	N	O		N	O	T	E	D		C	E	E

24 ■ The Whole Shootin' Match

C	R	E	S		S	W	I	S	S		M	F	R	S
H	E	L	I		I	O	N	I	A		O	L	I	O
A	S	E	C		G	O	O	D	Y	G	O	O	D	Y
L	O	C	K	I	N	F	R	E	S	H	N	E	S	S
E	L	T	O	N			S	O	I	R				
T	D	S		I	G	A	S		Z	I	L	C	H	
		I	N	A	S	P	O	T		S	I	L	O	
S	T	O	C	K	T	H	E	F	R	E	E	Z	E	R
I	O	W	E		E	Y	E	L	E	T	S			
R	A	N	D	R		D	A	S	H		P	Y	M	
			D	I	O	N			A	E	I	O	U	
B	A	R	R	E	L	O	F	M	O	N	K	E	Y	S
B	R	A	I	N	D	R	A	I	N		I	M	O	K
L	I	E	N		A	T	I	M	E		N	A	M	E
S	A	S	K		S	H	R	E	D		G	N	A	T

25 ■ Happy Endings

26 ■ 21st-Century Santa

27 ■ Airborne

28 ■ Last Gasp

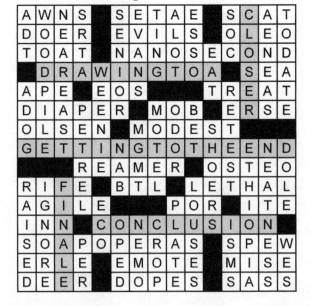

29 ■ *Phone-y Excuses*

```
I C A N   I T S O   B I L K O
M O J O   N O O K   E D E N S
A T O M   S T U B   D O N O T
M Y B A T T E R Y I S L O W
    A R A B   M D I I
    I M I N A D E A D Z O N E
B A S   M T G E   S E E O U T
E V I L   S C H   S H I A
R E T O S S   A O N E   E T S
I C A N T P U L L O V E R
    D R A T   Y S E R
    I M O U T O F M I N U T E S
S T A N D   P O O R   P I X Y
A I M E E   I B L E   T E E N
G N A R L   A S Y E   S A D E
```

30 ■ *Culture Club*

```
    E D I E   W E S T E R N
A R U G U L A   E N C A R T A
L O N G E S T   A D O P T E E
A D I O S   S T R U T   E S S
N E O N   M A R   P I A
S O N   P E T A L   A C M E S
    J O A N   P O I   T A V I
S T A R S A N D S T R I P E S
S I C S   T A O   S O I L
T S K E D   N O H O W   E S P
    R E F   R O N   A L K A
A R S   S A L S A   A L E U T
R E P L I C A   R A D I A L S
C L E A R E D   S N I F F L Y
S O C I E T Y   E I N E
```

31 ■ *Any Body Here?*

```
T O G A   R A B B I S   M C S
E A R P   A R R E S T   I O C
S T E P   H E A D H O N C H O
S H E L F   A D S   R A R E R
    N E A L     E E Y O R E
A R M S D E A L E R S   N E D
S N E E   S L I C E U P
P A N E L   O V A   P A T I O
    D I N N E R S   L O O K
S S E   L E G S D I A M O N D
T A N G L E   S L I D
A M T O O   R A P   I S L A M
F E E T O F C L A Y   T E R I
F A R   E R M I N E   R O T S
S S S   T Y P I S T   Y O Y O
```

32 ■ *After U*

```
D A T E   B H T   S H E B O P
U G H S   M A I   C A R R I E
H A U L L O G S   R E S U L T
S L R   E V E N S O   A N E T
    J O I N T C U S T O D Y
G I J A N E   A N T Z
A T E N   G E T G O   W E D
T U R N F O R T H E W O R S E
T P K   O N I C E   T A P A
    A T E E   C L I P O N
B O L T O F F A B R I C
U N I T   I S T L E S   M A S
R E L I E F   B O A T N E C K
M A L L E T   A O K   O M N I
A L E A S H   Y D S   V E E P
```

33 ■ Civics Class

M	E	R	V		A	B	A	B	Y		R	A	T	S
A	L	I	I		T	O	N	I	O		E	P	E	E
T	O	B	E		H	A	D	T	O		F	I	N	E
		T	H	E	T	W	O	H	O	U	S	E	S	
A	D	O	N	A	I	S			O	U	G	H	T	A
P	E	D	A	L	S		I	L	O	S	E			
P	R	I	M	E	M	I	N	I	S	T	E	R		
T	M	S			M	E	N				A	J	A	
	T	H	E	O	P	P	O	S	I	T	I	O	N	
	E	X	I	S	T		P	R	A	T	E	D		
G	O	S	P	E	L		S	H	O	R	T	L	Y	
O	F	P	A	R	L	I	A	M	E	N	T			
O	F	I	T		A	S	T	E	R		A	L	T	O
S	A	R	I		M	E	R	L	E		N	A	I	L
E	L	E	C		P	E	A	L	S		S	P	E	D

34 ■ What's Your Point?

H	A	H	A	S		P	U	T	I	N		C	S	I
A	D	O	P	T		A	T	O	N	E		O	T	S
S	A	T	I	E		P	U	S	H	B	R	O	O	M
	P	L	E	A		U	R	S	A		E	L	O	
S	T	I	C	K	M	A	N		L	A	L	A	L	A
H	O	P	E	S	O		G	E	M	I	N	I	S	
Y	R	S		N	E	E	R		O	C	T	E	T	
		H	A	T	T	R	I	C	K	S				
F	I	D	E	L		E	S	T	A		S	P	R	
A	T	E	L	E	S	S		R	O	M	P	E	R	
T	E	E	P	E	E		B	O	B	B	Y	O	R	R
	R	P	M		E	A	R	S		T	H	U	S	
S	A	F	E	T	Y	N	E	T		A	E	S	O	P
C	T	R		S	O	U	S	E		I	R	A	N	I
H	E	Y		O	U	T	T	O		N	O	L	A	N

35 ■ Behind Bars

N	A	M		C	R	E	P	T		C	A	P	T	S
E	T	A		R	I	C	H	E		O	R	I	O	N
W	O	R	K	I	N	G	O	N		S	E	N	N	A
T	R	I	O	S		T	H	E	M	A	T	I	C	
	J	A	I	L	H	O	U	S	E	R	O	C	K	
B	T	U		S	U	E		T	K	T				
O	R	A	L		G	A	S		S	I	T	T	E	R
N	O	N	O	S		T	H	E		C	H	O	R	E
E	N	A	M	E	L		A	N	G		O	B	O	E
		C	U	B		D	U	H		O	O	F		
P	R	I	S	O	N	E	R	S	S	O	N	G		
R	E	S	O	N	A	T	E		R	A	G	A	S	
I	L	I	A	D		C	H	A	I	N	G	A	N	G
G	E	T	M	E		H	A	L	V	E		N	O	T
S	T	A	I	D		A	B	E	E	T		S	S	S

36 ■ I Dream of Genie

A	H	A		I	T	S	S	O		T	H	I	R	D
R	E	P		C	R	E	P	T		H	O	S	E	R
T	A	P		S	A	R	A	H	P	O	L	L	E	Y
I	D	E	A		G	A	Y	E	R		D	A	V	E
	B	A	G	P	I	P	E		E	A	S	T	E	R
J	U	L	I	E	C	H	R	I	S	T	I	E		
A	T	T	N	S		S	A	T	O	N				
B	T	O		T	A	N		M	O	N		A	P	T
		M	E	R	C	I			I	G	L	O	O	
	G	O	R	D	O	N	P	I	N	S	E	N	T	
S	A	Y	S	S	O		L	E	N	G	T	H	Y	
E	T	R	E		U	R	I	A	H		S	O	T	O
A	W	A	Y	F	R	O	M	H	E	R		U	A	W
O	A	T	E	R		A	B	E	A	T		S	I	L
F	R	E	D	O		D	O	N	T	S		E	L	S

37 ■ 'Tis the Season

38 ■ It's Neapolitan

39 ■ Repeat After Me

40 ■ I Said, Repeat After Me!

41 ■ *En-abled Puzzle*

```
T A T E R . S I R E . V I S E
E T H N O . I D O L . I N T S
N O R T E . R E A L I S T I C
E M E R . S E E N E N O U G H
N B A . P A N . . G R I M E .
D O D G E D . P I E . . T A W
S M E A R . O I N K E D . . .
. B R O K E N E N G L I S H .
. . L Y R I C S . E N I A C .
B A S . . A T E . Y V O N N E
A R C D E . . I R E . A D E .
S E R E N E N E S S . A T M E
I T I N E R A R Y . S A R A N
C O P T . R U S E . S H A D E
S O T S . S T E T . E S S E N
```

42 ■ *Auto Motives*

```
L T D S . L A D I D A . B B C
A E R O . A D O N I S . A A H
D U A L A I R B A G S . R A E
. T W I T T E R . . O R B S .
M O N D E . P O W E R S E A T
O N E S E C . . I M E L D A S
D I A . A S I N I N E . . . .
. C R U I S E C O N T R O L .
. . T H I N K S O . . N E E .
O R L E A N S . R A N T A T .
F O U R D O O R S . M A H R E
F O T O . . I T S O P E N . .
I S I . F U L L Y L O A D E D
S T S . B R O L L Y . L O R E
H S T . I L L S E E . M T S T
```

43 ■ *Centre Pieces*

```
R U E S . A O R T A S . R S T
E N C L . D W A R F S . E T E
S A L A M A N D E R S . G I N
T R A V I S . I S A . O A F S
A M I E L . D I S M A N T L E
T E R R A C E . E L I T E S .
E D S . . Y E A H . T O A S T
. . M I D D L E M A N . . . .
A S M A D . S P A M . . T A S
S H A R E S . R E S C A L E .
P E R M A N E N T . P O R T A
H E R S . A L A . B U N T E D
A R Y . K I L I M A N J A R O
L E M . O L I V I A . O R E G
T R E . A S S E S S . B E D S
```

44 ■ *A Likely Story*

```
R U M O U R . B B L S . P I C
A S E N S E . R A I N G E A R
T O S E E D . A L O U E T T E
. S P R E A D I N G L I E S .
M A I M . Y E S . . . T I T .
I C E . F E R . B U L L E T S
S U S H I . R O L E O . . . .
. T E L L I N G F I B S . . .
. . S E E D S . . G E N E S .
C O W A R D S . D U H . O L E
A K A . . O R S . F W I W .
M A K I N G S T U F F U P . .
E Y E T O O T H . L I N E A R
T E N T P O L E . A L K A L I
O D S . E F O R . G O S S I P
```

45 ■ *Unhatched Chickens*

C	H	A	R	G	E		M	A	X		O	D	D	
H	O	B	O	E	S		D	O	S	E		H	E	Y
A	T	O	L	L	S		O	N	E	S	L	I	C	E
W	O	U	L	D	A		N	O	V		U	F	O	
E	N	N	S			T	R	E		C	O	R	E	
R	E	D	U	B	S		C	A	R	D	I	N	A	L
		P	A	S	M	O	I		W	E	L	T	S	
P	S	I		S	H	O	U	L	D	A		Y	E	E
A	C	T	A	S		U	N	S	E	R	S			
R	O	W	D	I	E	S	T		O	F	A	R	M	S
A	R	E	A		N	E	O			T	O	O	T	
	C	R	Y		S	T	N		C	O	U	L	D	A
T	H	E	S	A	U	R	I		U	N	P	L	U	G
H	E	S		A	R	A	T		E	T	O	I	L	E
O	R	O		H	E	P		D	O	N	E	E	S	

46 ■ *Well, Well, Well*

I	N	C	A	S		V	O	I	L	E		M	I	C
F	I	R	M	A		E	N	D	E	D		E	S	A
A	G	E	O	F		G	O	E	S	U	N	D	E	R
	H	A	V	E	Y	O	U	D	E	C	I	D	E	D
A	T	M	E		E	U	R			P	L	I	E	
M	O	P		D	S	T		M	B	A		E	T	D
S	W	I	P	E	D		E	C	O	N	O			
	L	E	T	M	E	T	H	I	N	K	N	O	W	
		S	O	A	R	S		E	L	O	P	E	D	
S	I	S		S	R	I		S	S	E		P	S	I
E	S	T	S			A	C	U		T	O	T	S	
T	H	A	T	S	A	S	U	R	P	R	I	S	E	
S	T	R	A	I	G	H	T	A		A	B	I	R	D
U	A	R		R	E	A	R	M		G	E	T	N	O
P	R	Y		E	D	G	E	S		A	R	E	S	O

47 ■ *Epitaph*

L	I	S	P		S	P	E	C	K		M	A	S	T
A	S	T	A		H	A	L	L	E		E	N	T	O
S	E	E	R		E	S	C	A	L	A	T	I	O	N
H	E	W	A	S	A	S	I	M	P	L	E	M	A	N
		S	H	R	E	D			I	R	A	T	E	
L	A	B	O	R	S			K	A	T	E			
O	V	U	L	E		D	E	N	Y		D	O	S	E
S	I	R		W	H	O	D	I	E	D		P	T	A
E	D	N	A		E	R	S	T		F	L	E	A	S
		C	R	A	M		S	L	E	D	G	E		
B	A	S	R	A		P	S	H	A	W				
O	F	C	O	M	P	L	I	C	A	T	I	O	N	S
M	O	O	N	S	H	I	N	E	R		S	T	A	N
B	O	N	Y		E	M	E	N	D		E	T	N	A
S	T	E	M		W	A	D	E	S		S	O	A	P

48 ■ *Tell Me the News*

G	E	A	R		C	L	A	S	P		M	I	L	A
A	L	P	O		M	O	P	E	Y		A	C	O	W
R	I	P	S	N	O	R	T	E	R		R	E	G	S
N	A	T	I	O	N	A	L	P	O	S	T			
I	S	S	E	T		L	Y	S		C	I	D	E	R
		S	A	B			N	O	N	A	M	E		
	O	T	T	A	W	A	C	I	T	I	Z	E	N	
C	F	L		S	H	A	L	T			E	R	E	
C	A	L	G	A	R	Y	H	E	R	A	L	D		
C	H	A	R	T	A			O	N	A				
I	D	S	A	Y		E	S	C		N	E	A	L	E
	V	A	N	C	O	U	V	E	R	S	U	N		
A	H	M	E		C	O	N	T	E	S	T	A	N	T
B	U	L	L		O	N	A	I	R		E	N	G	R
S	P	A	Y		S	O	R	T	A		S	A	S	E

49 ■ Northern Heroes

```
E R S _ I D E S _ C A P L E T
R O L Y P O L Y _ A L L U R E
I D E A S M A N _ R O A R E D
C A P T A I N C A N U C K _ _
A N T E _ _ _ W A D E _ _ _
_ _ S E A W A L L _ B R A S
A P B _ W H O S _ M O O L A
S E R G E A N T P R E S T O N
A L I A S _ R A Y S _ E E K
P E G S _ S T A R E A T _
_ _ M I T A _ _ A S K A
_ C A N A D I A N I D O L S
B O O I N G _ S T E M A R I E
L O O N I E _ T E X A S T E A
T O S S E S _ S E T S _ A G T
```

50 ■ Members of the Club

```
B M O C _ G A M M A _ G D A Y
R A V I _ A L E U T _ A U T O
I C O N _ T A L K T U R K E Y
T H I C K E _ I L E R _ E M O
S O D O I _ T S U N A M I _
_ _ D A M A S K _ N I T E S
A R N E _ E T A _ B U L O V A
R O O M I E S _ M O S Q U E S
C U S A C K _ M E A _ U T N E
O X E Y E _ I A G R E E _
_ D O M I N G O _ A T I C K
P S I _ A N N I _ I R O N O N
K E V I N B A C O N _ A T M O
W R E N _ E T A I L _ S W A B
Y A D A _ D E L L A _ T O S S
```

51 ■ Taking Turns

```
S C R A M _ M E G A _ G L A M
A L A D Y _ O N A C C O U N T
T O R A H _ R O O T H A I R S
O V E R A N E W L E A F _ _
R E S _ T A N _ _ S T O R K
I N T L _ M O P E D _ D I E
_ _ E R E _ E R E C T I N G
_ T H E O T H E R C H E E K _
P O O R M A R K _ L E T _
L I L _ G H A N A _ E A R N
O L E O S _ O R I _ H A I
_ _ B A C K T H E C L O C K
E X T E M P O R E _ A E R E O
D I E S E L O I L _ L O S I N
W I N E _ S L O P _ L I E N S
```

52 ■ Grey Areas in Math

```
P E P T O _ S T I N E _ O R T
A L E R O _ K U D O S _ H O O
T E N O F _ I T I N A _ S S T
R A N I S _ M O O S _ N U I T
I N A S _ P O R T _ C A R T E
O O M _ S A V _ S C H M E A R
T R E S T L E S _ L O A _
_ S Q U A R E R O O T S _
_ _ U N C _ R A N S H O R T
I N V I T E S _ S E E _ B O O
S U E R S _ O O P S _ M E S A
I M R E _ A R T I _ H E R E S
N E D _ T U T T E _ I T S A T
T R U _ O L I O S _ R O U T E
O O N _ I D E S T _ T O P E R
```

53 ■ Pucker Up

```
B L A B S . I N T O . C A P A
L E M O N . N O O R . O L I O
E C O L I . O U T O F L U C K .
W H O E V E R N A M E D I T .
. . R E L . S L E D S .
S C R O L L S . S O O N E S T
U R I . E A T . R A N T O
N E C K I N G W A S A P O O R
U P E N D . O N T . L R T
P E S E T A S . S A S H A Y S
. . E A R N A . I W O .
. J U D G E O F A N A T O M Y
F I R E S T O R M . I T H E E
A B L E . O T O S . N I N E S
R E S P . O S S O . S P O R T
```

54 ■ Menacing Puzzle

```
B A S I C . H E C K . D I G S
E A U D E . E L O I . A L O T
G R E E N K R Y P T O N I T E
S E D A T E . . A S A T E A M
. . . R C A . C H E . .
. D R F U M A N C H U . P J S
C R E E P I N T O . S L U E
S I L E N T T . O D D S A R E
I B E T . E L L I N G T O N
S S T . T E R M I N A T O R .
. . S I N . N O I . .
I N S E R T S . N I B B L E
K I T E E A T I N G T R E E S
I C E D . I L S A . S A N D S
D E W Y . L O A M . A N D S O
```

55 ■ Dollars and Cents

```
P A R T I . C O M M E R C E
E T H A N . M A D E A D E A L
R O O T S . O L D A S T I M E
M O N E Y D O E S N T . K E G
S T E R N O . . L I L Y
. . . C O M . T H E E .
F L O N . B U S Y A S A B E E
M A X I M I Z E P R O F I T S
S M O K E E A T E R . S O A P
. . O R S K . D I S .
K I L N . . E L P A S O
A R E . T A L K I T Y E L L S
B A G L A D I E S . D P L U S
O B O E R E E D S . O T E R I
B U S I N E S S . G O R S E
```

56 ■ Spin Cycle

```
M R T . S O R E L . A D E A R
E E W . T W I S T . T I N G E
W H O C A N S A Y . E S T E S
L A C Y . H U R R I C A N E
. S O C A N I . O N S I D E
S H A L L I . M O I . L A D
R E T O O L . A L L A T .
A S S N S . A N D . L O N G I
. . E S T E E . M A R O O N
O S O . A R T . I S N T O K
R A P P E R . A L T A R S .
W H I R L P O O L . D U E S
H A N O I . A T O M B O M B S
A R E S T . S H O U T . P A R
T A S T E . T O K Y O . S Y S
```

■ BARBARA OLSON & DAVE MACLEOD

57 ■ Disney Movies You Missed

58 ■ Making the Cut

59 ■ The Mane Concern

60 ■ Following Orders

61 ■ *Oh, Baby!*

S	R	S		M	I	D	S	T	S		A	S	S	T
P	E	C		A	S	C	O	O	L		N	A	N	A
O	W	E		C	A	L	F	M	U	S	C	L	E	S
O	O	N	A			A	M	M	O		A	E	S	
F	R	E	N	C	H	F	R	Y		M	A	D	R	E
S	K	I	A	R	E	A			V	E	R	B	A	L
			I	N	T	I	M	E		T	A	T	S	
		C	U	B	R	E	P	O	R	T	E	R		
A	S	A	N		I	D	O	T	O	O				
S	T	N	I	C	K		O	N	A	L	A	R	K	
P	A	A	V	O		K	A	R	A	T	E	K	I	D
E	S	D		N	A	N	U			B	I	O	L	
C	H	I	C	K	M	A	G	N	E	T		M	T	A
T	E	A	M		A	V	E	R	S	E		B	E	N
S	S	N	S		T	E	R	C	E	L		O	R	G

62 ■ *Phooey!*

C	A	P		B	A	H	A	I		U	S	E	A	S
A	L	I		A	B	O	R	C		P	L	A	N	T
H	U	E	Y	D	E	W	E	Y		T	A	R	D	E
I	M	P	A	S	S	E	S		C	A	T	T	L	E
E	N	A	T	E				T	A	L	K	S	H	O	P
R	A	N		E	A	T		L	E	E		D	U	E
			A	D	S	O	R	B		S	L	A	I	N
S	O	T	S		H	O	O	E	Y		E	Y	E	S
T	O	R	S	O		T	O	R	E	R	O			
T	E	E		U	Z	I		T	S	E		M	M	X
H	E	A	R	T	E	N	S		F	R	I	A	R	
O	B	T	U	S	E		H	A	C	I	E	N	D	A
M	A	I	N	E		K	E	R	B	L	O	O	E	Y
A	B	E	A	T		B	E	T	E	L		A	D	E
S	Y	S	T	S		S	T	I	R	S		N	O	D

63 ■ *Season Finales*

P	V	T		C	A	M	S		I	N	R	O	M	E
A	I	R		A	S	I	A		N	O	E	V	I	L
C	L	E	A	N	I	N	G		G	R	E	E	N	E
T	A	X	R	A	T	E		H	A	T	B	R	I	M
			I	D	I	O	C	Y		H	O	T		
C	R	I	S	I	S		H	E	Y		K	H	A	N
L	A	N	K	A		S	I	N	E		S	E	M	I
E	N	T		N	U	T	C	A	S	E		T	I	X
A	D	O	S		S	A	K	S		G	O	O	S	E
T	R	A	C		A	T	E		M	O	R	P	H	S
		C	A	T		E	N	A	C	T	S			
W	E	T	L	A	N	D		T	H	R	O	N	E	S
A	P	I	E	C	E		T	R	A	I	N	I	N	G
L	E	O	N	I	D		H	E	L	P		C	D	T
T	E	N	E	T	S		C	E	E	S		E	S	S

64 ■ *Banana Split*

B	A	N	G	S		S	M	U	G		E	R	M	A
A	T	A	L	E		U	R	S	A		M	E	A	L
R	E	G	A	L		P	E	E	N		P	I	C	S
B	A	N	D	A	G	E	D	I	G	U	A	N	A	
I	S	A	Y	S	O				T	E	N	N	E	R	S
E	E	G	S		M	L	A		S	P	A	D	E	S
			S	E	A	T	O		A	D	I	N	S	
	B	A	N	K	R	U	P	T	D	I	A	N	A	
M	A	D	E	A		D	A	T	E	D				
G	R	O	A	T	S		R	O	B		I	R	A	S
T	E	R	R	E	N	E		R	A	T	O	U	T	
	B	A	N	R	O	S	H	H	A	S	H	A	N	A
B	E	B	E		O	K	A	Y		P	A	R	T	I
B	A	L	S		P	I	M	P		I	C	E	I	N
C	R	E	S		S	E	S	E		C	A	R	E	S

65 ■ Purchasing Power

```
F R A N C   S K I D   O M S K
U N G E R   O I L Y   N O P E
L A R G E B I L L S   A N A G
    A V E R T     E D E N S
C O S T A S   I L L S A Y
U T M O S T   E Y E D R O P S
S T A R S   P S I S   E R O O
T A L   E V A   N S C   D I R
O W L S   A P I G   A L E N E
M A C H O M A N   B L U R T S
    H O O P L A   A L L S E T
S E A O F   S O R E L
O M N I   B A N K D R A F T S
S I G N   E D I E   I B A R S
O R E S   E S T D   D Y N E S
```

66 ■ Order, Order!

```
C A B L E   B H A T   A C C T
A S I A N   E A T A   B A I O
R I O T I N G M O B   O N N O
    E G O I S M   T V S E T
O O H   M I N T   V R O O M S
T O O F A R   E L I A   F A Y
I N R E   P R E V I E W
C A N A S T A   N E T L O S S
    E R O T I C A   S R T A
A S T   L O L L   B E E M E R
M I S H A P   A C E D   S P A
I N N E R   S T R A I T
D I E S   U T T E R C H A O S
S S S S   N Y E T   T E R R E
T E T E   S E R E   S O F E W
```

67 ■ The Moral of the Story

```
D I A   A M P U L E   I R O N
E T S   T A I P A N   M E N D
A L L W O R K A N D   A P O P
F L E E R   H A U N C H
E D E L   P I E R R E   R A S
N O P L A Y M A K E S J A C K
    P R O D   T O S E A
A C T U P O N   D I L B E R T
L O R N A   E I N E
A D U L L B O Y A N D J I L L
N E E   L A P E L S   I D E E
    B U S H E L   O M I N E
K I L N   A R I C H W I D O W
I T U P   M A D D E N   I R A
N S E C   A S S E T S   T E Y
```

68 ■ B-o-o-ring

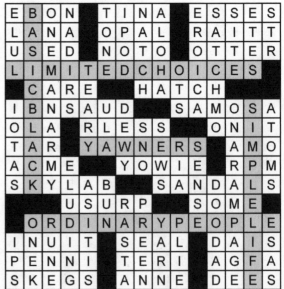

```
E B O N   T I N A   E S S E S
L A N A   O P A L   R A I T T
U S E D   N O T O   O T T E R
L I M I T E D C H O I C E S
  C A R E   H A T C H
I B N S A U D   S A M O S A
O L A   R L E S S   O N I T
T A R   Y A W N E R S   A M O
A C M E   Y O W I E   R P M
S K Y L A B   S A N D A L S
    U S U R P   S O M E
O R D I N A R Y P E O P L E
I N U I T   S E A L   D A I S
P E N N I   T E R I   A G F A
S K E G S   A N N E   D E E S
```

69 ■ *The Ins Are Out*

```
P S S T · I N H U M E · M P S
I T C H · S N A P O N · O A K
C U R E X P E N S E S · V S O
· B E N D Y · D T S · F E T A
A B A C I · I S A · D R O O L
W O M E N S T U I T I O N ·
H R E · T A P R O O M ·
O N R A M P · · A R M F U L
· M E A S L E S · I N E
· V E S T M E N T F U N D S
S T U N S · A T V · A N D E S
U R L S · E S P · S I T A R
M U G · U N H A B I T A B L E
A R A · T I E S I N · C L A D
C O R · A D D S O N · K E Y S
```

70 ■ *Don't Be a Brat*

```
S O W · A M B · S S T · M A W
T E E · G R O U P I E · A L E
A N E · I T S N O T M Y J O B
Y O D E L · O C T O P U S E S
· · D E R M O · N O M ·
P O D S · A S O F · · I S T
R U P E R T · P I T T A N C E
I T L L N E V E R H A P P E N
C R U S A D E R · R O T U N D
E E S · H A L O · E T E S
· · B O A · T O W N S ·
M A R I A C H I S · E T O N S
I D O N T H A V E T O · N A H
L E X · H O M E R U N · E M U
A N Y · S O S · S T S · S E T
```

71 ■ *Name-calling*

```
P A N T S · A B O · R C P T S
A L E R O · G I N G E R T E A
R O V E R B O O T S P O L L Y
S T E E R E R · H O L A ·
· · T E N A C E · A T A R I
· N O L T E A D O N I D A S
D C U P · L O S T A R T S
H A M · J E B · T H S · O O H
A M E N A B L E · T I N E
B E R O L B I C P I L O T ·
I L O N A · S T E N O S ·
· A P A T · D R A C U L A
A D A M E V E C A I N A B E L
I N G E N E R A L · E L E V E
R A T S O · S T S · R E R I G
```

72 ■ *Say "Cheese"*

```
H A V A R T I · A S S U R E
A N I S T O N · M O O R E D
D I S P E R S E · S A L I V A
A T E E · S I M S · M I S S M
· C H I N M U S I C ·
G R A T A · E N E · I M A C
O O F · B L O N D E · T A C O
U T A · S A N T A N A · Y U L
D O C S · R E H E A T · A R B
A R E A · C H A · I F S A Y
· U P H O L S T E R ·
B R A C E · P E T R · I L A Y
R E C I P E · R O A D G A N G
I G U E S S · I S A I D N O
E S P R I T · C H E D D A R
```

73 ■ It's a Mad Scramble

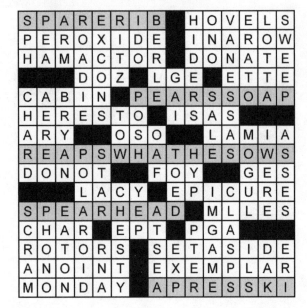

74 ■ In Living Colour

75 ■ Famous Last Words

MORE
O Canada Crosswords!

With their distinctive folk-art covers and uniquely Canadian content, the *O Canada Crosswords* books have garnered a devoted fan base of crossword aficionados from coast to coast. Spellings are Canadian too, and the words are derived from our history, geography and pop culture.

O Canada Crosswords, Book 1, 115 Great Canadian Crosswords • 8½ x 11, 136 pp, pb
978-1-894404-02-0 • $14.95

O Canada Crosswords, Book 2, 50 Giant Weekend-size Crosswords • 8½ x 11, 120 pp, pb
978-1-894404-04-4 • $14.95

O Canada Crosswords, Book 3, 50 More Giant Weekend Crosswords • 8½ x 11, 120 pp, pb
978-1-894404-11-2 • $14.95

O Canada Crosswords, Book 4, 50 Incredible Giant Weekend Crosswords • 8½ x 11, 120 pp, pb
978-1-894404-18-1 • $14.95

O Canada Crosswords, Book 5, 50 Fantastic Giant Weekend Crosswords • 8½ x 11 • 120 pp, pb
978-1-894404-20-4 • $14.95

O Canada Crosswords, Book 6, 50 Great Weekend-size Crosswords • 8½ x 11 • 120 pp, pb
978-0-88971-206-5 • $14.95

O Canada Crosswords, Book 7, 50 Wonderful Weekend-size Crosswords • 8½ x 11 • 120 pp, pb
978-0-88971-218-8 • $14.95

O Canada Crosswords Book 8, 75 Themed Daily-Sized Crosswords • 8½ x 11 • 176 pp, pb
978-0-88971-217-1 • $12.95